The neutral island facing the Atlantic,
The neutral island in the heart of man,
Are bitterly soft reminders of the beginnings
That ended before the end began.

Look into your heart, you will find a County Sligo,
A Knocknarea with for navel a cairn of stones,
You will find the shadow and sheen of a moleskin mountain
And a litter of chronicles and bones.

Look into your heart, you will find fermenting rivers,
Intricacies of gloom and flint,
You will find such ducats of dream and great doubloons of ceremony
As nobody today would mint.

But then look eastward from your heart, there bulks
A continent, close, dark, as archetypal sin,
While to the west off your own shores the mackerel
Are fat—on the flesh of your kin.

LOUIS MACNEICE, The Closing Album

## ACKNOWLEDGMENTS

In addition to the sources listed in the Bibliography I am particularly indebted to the following for advice, assistance and encouragement: Leo Daly; Dr John Fleetwood; Jarlath Hayes; Miss Kerry Holland, Archives Dept., University College, Dublin; George Holmes; Leslie Matson; Vincent Walker; Captain Peter Young, Army Press Office; the Irish Railway Record Society.

I am grateful to the following for permission to reproduce illustrations: Bord na Mona, (No. 3); Coras Iompair Eireann (20); Philip Conran (4); Department of Defence (6, 13, 35, 26, 34); G. A. Duncan, (1, 2, 7, 8, 10, 18, 22, 25, 29); Miss C. Kavanagh (24); Keystone (11, 15, 19, 21, 27, 30); M. O'Cassidy, (14); Eamon O'Rourke (31); Radio Times Hulton Picture Library (5, 9, 12, 16, 17, 28, 33); the cartoons used as chapter headings are reproduced from *Dublin Opinion* by kind permission of C. E. Kelly.

The quotation from *Neutrality* by Louis Macneice is reproduced by permission of Faber and Faber.

# CONTENTS

# *Introduction*

SOMETIME in the summer of 1939 I got stuck half way up and half way down the scree on the top of the Great Sugarloaf mountain in County Wicklow. The world suddenly seemed a big and lonely place, and, if this was not my first experience of the malignancy of nature, I don't remember any other. I burst into tears.

Barely nine at the time, I took little cognisance of the adult world, being far more interested in my first copy of *Meccano Magazine* which I had ordered (or perhaps I had ordered for me) from a little shop at the bottom of Hollybank Road, Drumcondra. It must, on second thoughts, have been myself, for it had the words 'little boy' on the back cover in pencil. For my sixpence I was introduced to a world of undreamed of delights, and to a great deal that was far beyond me. *Air News* informed me that the British transatlantic air mail service had been inaugurated successfully, the flying-boat *Caribou*, piloted by Captain J. C. Kelly-Rogers, having taken off from Southampton accompanied by the *Maia* to be welcomed at Foynes by a large crowd that included 'Mr de Valera, Prime Minister of Eire, who later watched from the *Maia* the mid-air refuelling of the flying boat by a tanker aircraft'.

If I knew little about flying boats, I knew even less about prime ministers. I was vaguely conscious of adult mutterings about obscure happenings in distant places, and a little more aware of the opinions of an uncle of mine—he must have been all of twenty-nine—who, reclining on a sofa, gave out about something I understood to be politics: but that is all I understood. By age, experience, and by the fact I was not to be in Ireland again until the Emergency was over, I am ill-equipped to offer a personal recollection of those exceptional years.

It would have been relatively easy to supply this deficiency. There are still very many people for whom the Emergency years are a vivid memory, perhaps the most vivid of their lives. But for this very reason an appeal to their assistance in attempting an impression of the period has certain major disadvantages. Firstly, the very vividness of those memories has produced some distortion and heightening, as I have several times ascertained through empirical methods. It is not just a matter of facts becoming confused as of hindsight operating to romanticise the ordinary, dramatise the humdrum, or apply an annealing process to the discrete fragments of day-to-day existence. Secondly, any narrative view of the period such as this sets out to be would inevitably become bogged down in a mass of unrelated detail.

I have therefore set out to present a picture of the Emergency years as reflected in contemporary or near-contemporary sources, amplified only in terms of verifiable fact and detail by the recollections of forty years on. Inevitably, and in consideration of the ground to be covered if anything approaching a balanced result is to be achieved, this has meant using a particular event or incident as symbolic of a general trend or pattern, a method which will not appeal to those who cherish their own particular memories and who remain convinced that their contribution to, or participation in, the events of 1939–45 was in some special way unique. This will obviously be most manifest in the case of civil defence; out of a mass of anecdote, recollection and documentation it is only possible, in a book of this scope, to select, and to select rigorously. Whole books can, and almost certainly will, be written on the basic subject matter of each of my chapters; some of them I would like to have written myself. But I have done my best to control my own inclination, as in, for example, the treatment of the transport situation, in the interests of a balanced survey.

I have, where possible, allowed individuals to speak for themselves, as there is frequently in the very choice of language and turn of phrase a strong evocation of an Ireland that has in many respects completely vanished. It was still a country in which everyone knew everyone else, in the sense that the actions of both groups and individuals—the Church, the IRA, Mr de Valera, *The Irish Times*, the Censorship of Publications, Jimmy O'Dea, the GAA—were to a large extent predictable and fully understood, if not necessarily condoned, by other groups and individuals.

External relations, with the exception of the continuing and anomalous relationship with Great Britain, did not exist for the mass of the people. Even before neutrality imposed its own quarantine it was an inward-looking society, a national village in which no one could walk down the main street without becoming the object of a multitude of keeking glances.

The modification of this national condition under the pressure of the events of the period is the theme of this book, in as far as it seeks to impose an interpretation upon facts and opinions. It is my conclusion that the Emergency period has contributed far more of a positive nature to the shaping of modern Ireland and the redefining of a national consciousness than has been generally acknowledged. Some of these contributions are tangible, and will be found set out in what follows. Others are in more debatable and less well-defined areas, and can only be briefly considered in this context. Together they constitute, however, an economic, social and political development which, though perhaps dormant in the years immediately following the Emergency, was to bear fruit in the early 1960s and thereafter.

There is one important fact that should be weighed against what follows. It is infrequently remembered, not only by antagonists abroad but by apologists at home, that Ireland was, at the period under review, a nation of less than three million people—you could have lost all of them in New York, London, Berlin, Rome or Tokyo—with a shaky history of less than twenty years of native government behind it. In this context even to have attempted a policy of neutrality with its inevitable consequences of political pressure and economic sanction, looks like a vast confidence trick. That it worked is still largely a matter for wonder and thanksgiving. Why it worked, and how it worked are the essential subjects of this record.

# *The closing album*

*... this is the people who once lent fire to an imperial race, whose genius flashed through two stupendous centuries of culture and success, who are now quietly receding into their own mists, turning their backs on the world of effort and action.*

EVELYN WAUGH, Put Out More Flags

*Everything here is perfectly abnormal: for the first time since the battle of Clontarf we are neutral.*

Dublin Opinion

THERE WAS flooding in Donnycarney. The overnight rain in the Dublin area had been accompanied by lightning and loud peals of thunder. The Seanad, recalled from the Summer recess the day before, had finally adjourned *sine die* at 4.50 a.m. on the morning of the third, having passed, with the minimum of protest, the emergency legislation presented to it by the Taoiseach, Eamon de Valera. 'I am voicing the opinion not of the majority but of quite a substantial section of the people in this country who are unhappy about this attitude of neutrality,' said Senator Sir John Keane. But he received little support. 'The part we are to play in the future is going to depend on the vitality which we display in a policy of neutrality', asserted Senator Patrick Baxter, elected on the Agricultural Panel. Neutrality, however, was still a baseless concept. The formulation of definitions and re-definitions was to last as long as the Emergency itself.

On the night of the second and third of September, 1939, the village of Pettigo, bisected by the border between Northern Ireland and what was then known under the 1937 Constitution as 'Eire, or in the English language Ireland' was half blacked-out. From eleven o'clock on the morning of the third the two halves of the village, and the two parts of the island of Ireland, were to go their separate political ways for the duration of what was a 'war' in the north, an 'Emergency' in the south. The Constitution had, in fact, presented Mr de Valera, its principal begetter, with both a problem and the opportunity for coining what was perhaps the first great euphemism of the century. The Constitution spoke only of peace and war; there were no grey areas. Dev. was equal to it. 'My view is that "a time of war" as defined in the Constitution, covers an emergency of this sort, an emergency such as we are now facing', he told the Seanad on the night of 2–3 September, in his Second Reading speech on the First Amendment of the Constitution Bill. It was an acceptable interpretation in the circumstances. 'I move that Seanad Eireann hereby resolves, pursuant to sub section 3 of Section 3 of Article 8 of the Constitution,' said Senator William Quirke, 'that, arising out of the armed conflict now taking place in Europe, a national emergency exists affecting the vital interests of the State.'

Thus the second of the two basic concepts had been established, on an equally empirical basis. That Sunday afternoon in Croke Park, Dublin, 39,307 people saw Kilkenny beat Cork 2–7 to 3–3 in the All Ireland Hurling Final. 'There is no reason for panic, or even for excessive fussiness' admonished *The Irish Times* the next morning, the first working day of the Emergency. Refugees were arriving from Britain in a generally well-ordered manner, though they were not allowed to bring their gas-masks ashore. Those arriving in Galway, however, had no gas-masks to bring. They were the 430 survivors, including ten stretcher cases, from the liner *Athenia*. The 'armed conflict' elsewhere moved a little nearer. Messrs G. D. Grannel, Building Contractors and Steel Erectors, of 65 Cadogan Road, Fairview, Dublin claimed to be the first in Ireland to advertise Air Raid Shelters, and announced practical demonstrations by appointment. Pullars the Cleaners, of St Stephen's Green, Dublin offered to dye old materials and curtains for the 'Black Out'—the term was still unfamiliar enough to demand the inverted commas. Mr P. Fitzsimons, Chairman of Navan Urban Council, claimed the knowledge of three million gas masks stored in Dublin ready for distribution in any emergency—with a small 'e'. The existence, or non-existence, of emergencies within the Emergency was to be repeatedly debated in political and other circles in the years to come.

The album was closing. On 6 September Joseph Connolly was appointed Controller of Censorship. On the eleventh a permit system was introduced regulating travel between Ireland and Great Britain. The price of fish went up, because, ironically enough, of a reduction in landings from Britain. There were 1549 fishing vessels on the Irish register. The Emergency Powers Control of Prices (No. 1) order came into operation, fixing prices as ruling on the previous 26 August, and coupled with a severe warning against hoarding. The Great Northern Railway, one of the dwindling lines of communication with the non-Emergency world, cancelled its Health and Pleasure trips to Clones. B & I services to Liverpool and other British ports were suspended indefinitely because of a dispute over War Risks pay. The London Midland and Scottish Railway's mailboat service continued to run from Dun Laoghaire to Holyhead, and on Tuesday 12 September fifty members of the German colony in Ireland left on board the *Cambria*, several of them to answer the call to arms. They were seen off by Herr Edouard Hempel, the German Minister in Dublin, and many of them carried bouquets of red roses. One little boy was dressed in a German naval uniform.

> In nineteen thirty nine or so
> The Emergency began to grow
> And Dev he says to me 'What ho!
> You're just the man for me!'
> Why Dev, sez I, why, so I am!
> We may be running short of ham
> And petrol, coffee, tea and jam,
> And ships that go to sea!

Mr de Valera, in his address to the nation, had announced cabinet changes and the setting up of a Department of Supplies under Mr Seán Lemass. On the same day that the new Minister announced that petrol rationing was to be introduced, Cork undertakers sent him a telegram demanding special concessions, an omen of the many difficulties that were in store for him. On Saturday 16 September a group of IRA members and sympathisers, including the writer Mairtín O Cadhain, were arrested under the Offenses against the State act and detained in the Curragh and the Bridewell. 'We all know that there is a body in this country with arms at its disposal', Mr de Valera told the Dáil. 'We know that in the last year its activities have taken a new turn, that the body has definitely proclaimed itself as entitled to exercise the powers of government here, to act in the name of our people, even to commit our people to war.' But the people had been committed, had committed themselves, said the politicians and the press, not to war, but to a National Emergency, the shaky cornerstone of which was a policy of neutrality. 'We're neutral,' declared *Dublin Opinion*, 'so we can't be such a green isle!'

It wasn't to be quite as simple as that.

3

"Oh, very good, Miss Murphy ! . . . The customer will not be right till after the emergency."

# Neutral against whom?

*Our neutrality towards other nations is not the declaration of an unfriendly intention but the asseveration of a natural right. The distinction, from every point of view, is important. It is our first practical claim to independence.*

The Bell

*If Britain is beaten in this war through lack of assistance that Ireland might give or get from her, we will have no self-esteem left as a nation, except that false self-esteem that has been so destructive to us already; Cheer up anyway! We may never really be found out—and we may some time develop a certain amount of natural gumption.*

GENERAL RICHARD MULCAHY in a letter to
J. M. KENNEDY

FOR THE plain people of Ireland, shortly to be relentlessly memorialized by the pen of Myles na gCopaleen, neutrality was primarily a negative condition—the absence from everyday life of the uncomfortable phenomena of armed conflict. It seemed enough to state the case for it to be accepted and proved acceptable. It had been stated in essence by Mr de Valera many times preceding the actual outbreak of hostilities, so that it came as a surprise to no one and even, in the early days of the so-called 'phoney war', appeared to have been accepted in circles which might have been expected to have been most critical. 'From the British point of view,' wrote the

London *Times* on 9 September 1939, 'it is more than probable that Eire's neutrality is the best possible policy that Mr de Valera's government could have adopted.'

The treaty ports had been evacuated by the British the previous year, and the outcry demanding their re-occupation, either by agreement or force, had yet to attain substantial proportions. Amongst those in Ireland concerned with the theory rather than the plain fact of neutrality, the weight of opinion was in favour. The first Emergency issue of *TCD*, the weekly undergraduate journal of an institution not then widely recognised for its nationalist viewpoint, caused some surprise and a certain amount of consternation when its editorial of 26 October baldly stated that Cromwell's England dealt with the Catholic Irish in the same energetic manner that Hitler reserved for the Jews. 'It is, we learn, bad taste for the Irish to refer to this . . .' the writer commented. He went on: 'Those of us who are not glad to be in neutral Ireland will, we hope, speedily depart to help whichever belligerent they favour. Most of us, however, are heartily glad to be outside, if only just outside, the tremendous futile catastrophe.' The anonymous editor, to be revealed the following term as one Conor Cruise O'Brien, was subsequently taken to task by those in the College who saw Ireland's role in a different light. 'No doubt we are glad that the British are going to the front for us', wrote R. B. D. French, 'but need we be smug about it?'

The climate of uncertainty reflected more than a moral dilemma. Ireland's legal right to assume neutrality, apart altogether from her ability to sustain it, was by no means universally recognised. Churchill later referred to Southern Ireland (his insistence on geographical rather than political terminology is in itself significant) as a State which was 'an undefined and unclassified anomaly'. 'I do not personally recognise Irish neutrality as a legal act', he wrote in *The Grand Alliance*. Though the language was legal the impetus was emotional. Britain's disentanglement from its oldest colony has been a long-drawn-out and reluctant process; even in 1977 a writer in the radical *New Statesman* cheerfully claimed Samuel Beckett as British, and other vestiges of cultural, if not political colonialism persist. In 1939 the young Irish state was barely 17 years old and still, to many British eyes and in spite of the 1937 Constitution, a spiritual, if not a physical part of the United Kingdom. Neutrality could be accepted on the part of other small nations such as Switzerland or Norway, but Irish neutrality was seen as an affront, a case of filial ingratitude if not outright insubordination. It was against this background that the country took up a position which was to bristle with difficulties on both the theoretical and practical level. 'The policy of neutrality is not by any means an easy policy and it is not a cowardly policy . . .' Mr de Valera was to say; 'It may be a more difficult policy, in the long run, than any other policy'. He was not overstating the case.

The concept, on a practical level, seemed perfectly possible in those early days.

There was no television to hurl the happenings in Poland into the sitting room. Aeroplanes were sporting contraptions unlikely to prove a serious embarrassment. The British navy, it was assumed, would not be interested in allowing an armed invasion to reach Irish shores, and the idea of airborne landings was too ridiculous to merit serious consideration. 'What possible invasion can there be of our frontiers?' James Fitzgerald-Kennedy asked in the Dáil; 'There can be none. Who is going to land a force here? Is it Great Britain or France? Is it against them we are arming? It is too nonsensical for words. Is it against Germany we are arming? How is Germany to send troops over here? Is she to beat the British navy from off the seas in order to land her expeditionary force here or are they to be dropped by aeroplanes? That is equally absurd.'

There was another kind of absurdity in some people's eyes: trying to suggest that our neutrality could be substantiated by a display of armed force. The essentially negative quality of the condition appealed to many: lie low and say nothing and maybe the whole horrible business will simply pass us by. A TD from Kilkenny, Denis Gorey, could not for his part even accept the necessity for air raid precautions. 'It is simply aping and playing', he told the Dáil, 'trying to attract notice instead of trying to be neutral'. For de Valera this attitude represented the greatest danger of all. 'Our greatest danger here is our complacency ... a complacency begotten by the fact that in the past we had not to defend ourselves directly, as that reponsibility lay with another people and another country.' The fact slowly began to sink in that, for the first time in seven hundred years Ireland was on her own.

In the debates in the Dáil and Seanad on the eve of the outbreak of war the Opposition, both Fine Gael and Labour parties, had pledged their support to the Fianna Fáil government and its leader. Fine Gael, though by tradition pro-British and a supporter of the vestigial Imperial link, had little choice but to accept the position. The support for a policy of neutrality, for good reasons and bad, was nearly unanimous, and to oppose it would be to court political extinction as well as gravely detrimental to the national interest. There were private reservations, however, and some outspoken statements of a divergent view. Frank McDermot suggested to the Seanad that Ireland's entering the war (on the allied side) would mean a practical co-operation in the defence of the 'British Isles' as a whole, and on the shipping vital to the country's survival. He also believed that the moral effect of its standing out of the war would be bad. Sir John Keane felt that Ireland's place was with the other Dominions, even though, in Churchill's view, she had repudiated Dominion status. He also recognised a moral dimension and brought in the question of Partition. 'It is not because we are a member of the Commonwealth at all, but because we feel so deeply the issues involved that we are prepared to declare ourselves as siding openly with the democracies', he told his fellow Senators. 'I believe we would do more in that act alone to unite our country and break down the unfortunate barriers that now divide it.' That was a card that was to be repeatedly played by the British and, later, the Americans, in their efforts to dismantle Irish neutrality.

'We are neutral here', said de Valera, 'but I do not think there is a single individual in this country at the moment who is neutral.' He went on to explain the apparent causistry, and to justify on its basis the imposition of a news censorship which shocked the visiting Ernest Bevin from Britain by its severity. Loyalty to Ireland was a complex phenomenon; some saw in England's difficulty Ireland's opportunity, and believed in a German victory as the best way to hasten the Republican millennium. Others, a dwindling but still influential minority, were, though physically in occupation of decaying country houses and other crumbling enclaves, not really living in contemporary Eire at all. 'They talk of *our* Navy and *our* Air Force, meaning those of England', wrote W. J. White (later to be Features Editor of *The Irish Times* and Director of Programmes for RTE) in his period as editor of *TCD*. Though a great number of them had done what they saw to be their duty and joined the British forces, 'the ones who have remained hold an anomalous position ... they join the American chorus of condemnation of Irish neutrality, accusing us of allowing others to fight our battles and of neglecting selfishly the good of humanity. What they do not do is join "their" forces.' The undergraduate editor went on to speculate what would be the attitude of those who had compromised by joining the volunteer Local Defence Force to an attack (the probability of which appeared at times to be nigh) by Ireland's nearest neighbour. 'Will they break their allegiance and refuse to obey orders, at the risk of being shot, or will they take up arms and fight against their brethren?' This intriguing question was destined not to receive an answer, but it continued to be asked. A former British army Major who had served in the 1914–18 war offered his services to assist in training the LDF. He was informed that he must be prepared to defend his country against any aggressor. He answered that he would, against any except the British. He was told to 'carry on'.

That may have been unofficial reaction, but there was concern, too, at higher levels. 'The Government mentality with regard to Britain and Northern Ireland is fantastic', complained General Richard Mulcahy, President of Fine Gael and one of their members on the Defence Conference which was composed of representatives from both the Government and the Opposition and was set up in May 1940. On 16 June in the same year, the 36th anniversary of Bloomsday, Mulcahy and his colleagues James Dillon and T. F. O'Higgins met Mr de Valera, Frank Aiken, who was in overall charge of Defence, and the Tánaiste and Minister for Finance, Seán T. O'Kelly, in discussions on Ireland's defence policy, or lack of it, which lasted from 4–6 p.m. Mulcahy had felt that the Defence Conference was 'without a background of reality', since they were rarely permitted to discuss other than marginal issues, and he gleaned little further satisfaction from his meeting with the Taoiseach and his colleagues. He came away with the impression that the Government's policy was that any invader, British or German, would be fought and that their belief was that if the British were to come in they would not leave again. He added a note to his memorandum of the meeting: 'If the Prime Minister is stating this as their outlook and the policy could be believed, then this country is being run by a mad dog.'

Fine Gael were clear enough in their own minds as to the necessary distinction to be made between potential invaders. They would resist a German attack in the expectation of the arrival of British assistance but, in the case of British aggression, they would find it impossible to recommend the continuance of military resistance. It was, of course, impossible to say this in public. De Valera told Mulcahy in November 1940 that there was a fundamental difference between their attitudes but that it would be 'a great disaster if it got out'. Mulcahy and his colleagues agreed, if for varying reasons. 'Our duty is to act as a brake or anchor on the Government', James Dillon wrote to the General, 'holding them back from plunging over the abyss of war with England.' The course of duty, and enlightened self-interest, was plain.

Irish myth has a habit of proving stronger than mere reality. 'Ireland is known to have a heavy rainfall and consequently low clouds and very frequent damp and foggy weather', Admiral Raeder reported to his Führer on 3 December 1940. Hitler, who had other things on his mind, apparently decided to invade Ireland only on request—from the Irish. During the previous summer he had ordered his information media to spread the story that a German invasion of Ireland was imminent, and it was believed both in the Swiss Chalet Restaurant, Merrion Row Dublin and in more conventional intelligence centres in Britain, where contingency plans were in readiness.

Following the Dunkirk evacuation Britain's General Montgomery had been asked to prepare plans for the seizure of Cobh, and, inevitably, Cork, for use as a naval base in the anti-submarine war in the Atlantic. De Valera hazarded, probably correctly, that the belligerents' sole interest in Ireland was as a base from which to fight each other. Thus, against what others saw as irrefutable evidence, he refused, throughout the course of the Emergency, entirely to dismiss the possibility of invasion from either side. This attitude infuriated many people. In January 1941 European news media were predicting a British invasion of Ireland, and the Bishop of Derry sent a priest to the Taoiseach to inform him that they intended attacking across the Border. But two months later General Mulcahy returned in a state of irritation from a conference with the Chief of Staff. 'Laboured suggestions were made about details of a possible British invasion from the north . . .' he noted. Mr de Valera, who was present throughout the three hour meeting, confessed to James

Dillon that he found it very difficult to concentrate after an hour or so. He had, after all, heard all of it before.

The rumours, which had begun with the declaration of the Emergency, were to continue, each one demanding some redefinition of neutrality as the possibilities rearranged themselves and the Americans replaced the British as the putative fire from the north. The fundamental concept, as conceived by de Valera, promulgated by his spokesmen and accepted, with a complexity of reservations, by the bulk of the population, was bluntly expressed by Mr Aiken in the United States in 1941: 'We are neither pro-German, nor pro-British, we are just pro-Irish'. If this was too simplistic, the analysis by the American Minister in Dublin, David Gray, was more so: 'He is not pro-German, not personally anti-British, but only pro-de Valera', he said of the Taoiseach, for whom he was developing growing antipathy. Mr de Valera himself, for those who had cared to listen, had expressed quite clearly the relationship between theory and practice in a Dáil speech on the 29 September 1939: 'Our attitude we hope to keep, not by adherence to some theoretical, abstract idea of neutrality or anything like that, but by addressing ourselves to the practical question that we do not want to get involved in this war, and we merely want to keep our people safe from such consequences as would be involved by being in this war.'

The practical question would demand some fine adjustments to the general theory.

NEUTRAL STATION.

"But this suit has been turned already, sir?"
"I know; I want it turned back."

# *Interlude: sleaghan agat!*

*My feet are here in Clonsast, this lonely maytime morn,*
*But oh the ache that's in me for the place where I was*
*born!*
*My back is nearly broken from toiling at the peat,*
*But oh, to back a horse today, in a well-known Dublin*
*street!*

*But here I am in Clonsast,*
*With footing turf my load,*
*And all these miles from Dublin*
*On the Old Bog Road!*

Dublin Opinion

'IF BRITAIN completely shuts off coal and gasoline', David Gray, the US Minister, wrote to President Roosevelt, 'this place would be a disorganised and howling wilderness in three months . . . It probably would be a wise thing to do to explode this nationalistic dream of "self-sufficiency" . . .'

One man's nationalistic dream is another man's foresight. The policy of industrialisation under the protection of a tariff wall which had been the policy of the State since the first Fianna Fáil government of 1932 had had its critics. But it had succeeded in creating a minimal industrial base virtually from nothing, and, if falling far short of 'self-sufficiency' it continued to provide a fitful supply of consumer goods of one kind and another throughout the Emergency period.

One thing that could not be confected in a back-street factory, however, was fuel and its equally essential by-product, power. The public were quick to get the message. On 5 September 1939, the second working day of the Emergency, Dublin coal offices were forced to close their doors at 1 p.m. as a result of panic buying. Two days later *Quidnunc* in *The Irish Times* speculated gloomily about the likely return of the Dublin trams, which had begun to disappear from the streets in favour of buses. On Monday 11 September the price of coal went up by two shillings (10p) a ton. And as the international situation worsened, so did the domestic fuel situation, aggravated by Churchill's covert economic policy of allowing Mr de Valera to 'stew in his own juice'. The effects on public and private transport are considered elsewhere. For the ordinary citizen, however, particularly the city dweller, it was the failure, or near failure, of gas, electricity and coal supplies which bit deepest.

The Electricity Supply Board, never an organisation to adopt a kid-glove attitude towards its customers, made little attempt to sugar the pill. '*No Electric Heating*' it announced in 1942: '*No Extra Electricity for Cooking*. 50 per cent of your *daily* consumption of this period last year for water heating. 10 per cent off motive power. 25 per cent off lighting and other uses.' Meter-reading became a skilled art. At this time the bulk of the ESB's current was generated in coal-fired power stations; had it not been for the existence of the Shannon hydro-electric scheme, reviled as a white elephant not long before, the situation would have been much worse. As it was, it was bad enough. There were further electricity restrictions in 1944, and the Board's approach to the consumer remained uncompromisingly heartless. 'The Electricity Supply Board has for sale to electricity consumers (who else?) a limited number of modern electric fires of the reflector type' it announced portentiously late in the same year. But the prospect of extended warmth faded rapidly with the ensuing proviso. 'To prevent any increase in the consumption of electricity', the announcement continued, 'sales will be made on the condition that the consumer surrenders at the time of purchase, *and at no value*, (my italics), an obsolete or inefficient fire. The consumer can purchase a new fire of the same or less loading than the fire surrendered and must bring his Electricity Ration Card with him when making his purchase.' Even the note of male supremacy (this was well before the time when the obscure Monsieur Chauvin began to earn himself a second reputation) was not missing. But, for the Dublin citizen at least, even getting his obsolete or inefficient fire to the ESB offices presented problems. The Dublin trams had finally succumbed to the electricity shortage in August 1944:

> The last tram is gone from the Pillar:
> Poor Nelson, alas, must have qualms!
> A sailorly cuss, who would not 'miss the bus',
> He must surely be missing the trams!

# The Importance of POTATOES!

The drastic reduction in the importation of human and animal foodstuffs renders essential a greatly increased production of home-grown food. An increased acreage of Potatoes is particularly important because POTATOES

☛ **ARE AN IDEAL AND INDISPENSABLE HUMAN FOOD**

☛ **PROVIDE EXCELLENT FEEDING FOR ALL TYPES of FARM STOCK including POULTRY**

☛ **YIELD FAR MORE FOOD PER ACRE THAN ANY OTHER CROP**

☛ **CAN BE SUCCESSFULLY GROWN IN ALL PARTS OF THE COUNTRY**

## ORDER YOUR SPRAYING MATERIALS EARLY!

## PLANT MORE POTATOES

*Issued by the Department of Agriculture*

K.A.A.

and of course there was no petrol for the private individuals, few at the time, who ran cars. No use hoping to pour out your frustrations to a sympathetic ear, either: phone calls, though still reasonably priced at twopence ($\frac{1}{2}$p) were restricted in January 1944 to a maximum of six minutes' duration. What saving that achieved is a matter for speculation.

The Emergency threw up its quota of national bogeymen, amongst whom could be numbered Tillage Inspectors, Tobacconists, Warble Fly Inspectors and Glimmer Men. 'Look out missus, here's the glimmer man!' echoed from street to street as that individual arrived, tight-lipped, to lay hands on your jets to see were they still warm. And if they were, you could expect no mercy and the bleak prospect of cold dinners.

Gas, produced from solid fuel, supplies of which had dwindled to all but a trickle, was savagely restricted, and what there was—the 'glimmer'—would take an hour or more to boil a kettle of water to pour over the recirculated tealeaves. By 1943 the country was operating on 16 per cent of its gas coal requirements (the comparative figures for tea and petrol were 25 per cent and 20 per cent respectively). All these commodities were, of course, imported, except for small supplies of Irish anthracite. A British cabinet sub-committee which in 1942 recommended 'keeping Eire's economy going on a minimum basis' (Britain was then the only feasible source of essential raw materials) appeared to be succeeding in its aim.

There was one fuel resource, however, about which the British could do nothing. Turf (officialese was later to prefer the rootless term 'peat') was available, in theory, in large quantities in midland and western areas of the country and in the Dublin and Wicklow mountains. In an era of cheap coal it found little favour in the cities, certainly in Dublin, and though the Turf Development Board had been set up in 1934 its progress in developing this native resource had not been spectacular. The situation had now changed dramatically, and the once-despised fuel became eagerly sought-after, if not so eagerly welcomed by the city housewife, who found its response to the customary fire-lighting ritual wayward to say the least. On 27 June 1941 the Parliamentary Secretary to the Minister for Finance was placed in overall control of the Turf Development Board, with instructions to use every means to stimulate maximum production, but the Board did not get around to issuing its 3d (1p) booklet *The Use of Turf as a Domestic Fuel* until 1944, long after most people had learnt the hard way. 'Why did it not appear four years ago?' demanded *The Bell*. In the previous year the Hammond Lane Foundry, who had presumably been working for some time on the project, had announced their 'Nu Turf' range, 'specially designed to burn turf scientifically and economically'. The trouble was that the turf available was neither scientific nor economic. In its natural state in the bog it contained anything up to 96 per cent water, and after for the most part being hand-won by the laborious traditional methods, the quantity was little diminished—some suggested, in fact, that it had been significantly augmented. The tradition of the country cottage turf fire that never went out remained largely a legend to the urban amateur.

And the hands of many an amateur turf-winner attested to its intractable and punishing qualities. Michael O'Beirne went for a month on the bog as a volunteer. 'The footing plots were like harrowed fields, with thirty-three rows to a field. Closer, the turf looked like enormous strips of toothpaste lying close together, spewed from a machine.

'An east wind blew across the bog. It had been raining; the turf was soft as mud. In the misery of handling the shapeless stuff I soon forgot the wind.

' "How are you getting on?"

It was the manager.

"Slowly, I'm afraid. My wrist got sprained—"

"H'm. Swollen? You've got thorlock: that's what they call it hereabouts. Let me know if it gets worse!"

'It got worse. I could only use one hand. So when the week was over, having footed half a plot thus earning 8/6d (42½p), I was changed to time work, at 8d (3p) an hour. This meant carrying the surveyors' instruments and doing various labouring jobs.'

There were civilian volunteers like O'Beirne. There were those who hired a turf bank and dug their own. And there was the Army. In 1944 the prize for the best developed bog worked by an Army unit, put up by the Turf Development Board, was won by the 31st infantry battalion stationed on the bog at Nadd, Co. Cork. But Army involvement had begun in 1941, when the forces acquired the necessary bogs and equipment. This was not entirely a simple matter, as most of the accessible bogs were in civilian hands, there were no powers of compulsory acquisition, and the Army had thus to be content with areas which required very extensive drainage and road-building to make them workable. By 1944, however, many units were providing for all their fuel requirements, though under some protest. 'The programme confronting our Division in the immediate future certainly lacks nothing in variety' announced *Spearhead*, the 2nd Division's journal, in May 1943: 'The biggest task, turf cutting, does not look like a military job at all. One can understand the grouse of the average soldier when he says he did not join the army to cut turf . . .'

Accommodation was under canvas, and, apart from the hard physical labour involved, the camps in the middle of nowhere offered few amenities. The Army, however, rose to the occasion. Captain McGoldrick of the Curragh Camp invented a new turf-cutting machine, which was at work on Lullymore bog during the 1941 season. 'It will cut a single slab of turf containing up to 80 sods' reported the *Curragh Bulletin*. 'It can be operated by 6 men or can be adopted (sic) for working by a horse and abolishes the necessity for sleansmen. The machine can be used for three operations—topping, cleaning and digging.' Even with such sophisticated mechanical aids, however, the troops of the Curragh Command must have been glad of the scarves, scarf helmets, pullovers, socks, gloves and mittens knitted for them by Mrs Esther O'Grady of Holloden, Muine Bheag, Co. Carlow and her band of enthusiastic lady helpers.

As the Emergency wore on the work became no easier, but life in the camps took on a slightly less spartan complexion. In April 1944 plans were ready for a complete programme of 'bog entertainments' for troops of the 2nd Division and Eastern and Western Commands. Emphasis was being laid, it was reported, on the distinction between 'Bogway Melodies' and the ordinary Barrack Variety. Run by a voluntary organisation called Defence Entertainments Travelling Shows (or DETS for short: enter the acronym) two shows went on tour covering the Eastern and Western command areas. The artistes were booked on a professional basis, and included a band and what was described as 'a chorus lineup of girls . . .'

The Dutch journalist Kees Van Hoek followed one such show to its destination: 'Our car meandered through a maze of high-walled Kildare by-roads, dappled with showers of gold sunspots through the young green of trees in Spring, trying to trail the bus which was bringing the Army Road-Show. "True", said a rustic sage in Clane, "I have seen a bus pass, a queer one, with a funny machinery trailing behind and full of soldiers and blondes." We caught up with the blondes, followed the bus, churning the dust, deep down the last and narrowest lane and there, along the bank of the Grand Canal, lay the camp.'

Meanwhile the piles of turf in Dublin's Phoenix Park grew higher. 'I'd like to rise from the ashes *that* would make,' as the Phoenix said.

Myles na gCopaleen revealed in *Cruiskeen Lawn* that he had been consulted by the Dublin City Manager, the Managing Director of the Gas Company and the Chairman of the Electricity Supply Board on the problem of conserving fuel. His solution was simple: a plan for lighting the streets by sewer gas. A mechanism built into a lampost would refine, vapourise and ignite it, and it would burn with a brilliant and odourless orange flame. He never saw, he told his readers, three men go out with a lighter step.

POSTAL CENSORSHIP OFFICE

# *Living and partly living*

*It was as if a whole people had been condemned to live in
Plato's cave, backs to the fire of life and deriving their only
knowledge of what went on outside from the flickering
shadows thrown on the wall before their eyes by the men and
women who passed to and fro behind them.*

F. S. L. LYONS

*I greet you from a neutral country in a neutral hour
When the blood pace slows and nothing stirs
But the leaves in the parks, so gently;
So gently that not even the newspaper headlines
Can fluster the plumes of swans gliding, gliding,
As on a lake of fire, fringed by pink water.
The pulse of life is faint, as in a trance,
As we await the backwash of hate's last outrage.*

ROBERT GREACEN

ROBERT GREACEN, the Ulster poet, arrived in Dublin from Belfast in 1943
and found it 'the most fascinating city in these islands . . . an oasis of light in
the surrounding gloom'. He met all the leading literary figures and set up the
New Frontiers Press which published a slim volume, *On the Barricades*, containing
work by himself and two other young poets of promise, Valetin Iremonger, later to
be ambassador successively to Sweden, India, and Luxembourg, and Bruce

Williamson. At this time *The Bell*, edited by Seán O Faoláin, was nearly three years old. 'This magazine will be creative only in so far as Ireland is creative. Only the people can create an image of themselves', he had pronounced in tones of dogmatic tautology in the first issue. 'This is Ireland young and earnest.'

It has become fashionable, indeed it had become fashionable during the period itself, to label Emergency Ireland as a forgotten backwater in which such creative talents as there were withered and rotted under the corporate influences of isolation, censorship and puritanical religion. 'The bleakness and meanness of material life in wartime, even on an island of peace, were matched by emotional and intellectual impoverishment. In a society already small, inward-looking and self-absorbed, the general, compulsory and unheroic isolation reinforced all that was static or retrogressive in its composition'—Oliver MacDonagh's strictures may be taken as fairly representative of this popular attitude. It became popular and has remained so for two reasons. One, there was a certain amount of truth in the assertions. Two, it was in the interest of certain people that it should be generally accepted. There are always those, unable to realise what they consider to be their creative potential, who will blame external conditions rather than face up to personal inadequacy; and Emergency Ireland had its share of these. From the external point of view the conclusion was based not so much upon demonstrable fact as upon wishful thinking. To the British in particular, it was inconceivable that a people who had in their eyes opted out could retain any dynamic whatsoever, and a snap judgement born largely of pique became thus accepted as a mature analysis. The view was not, however, confined only to the disaffected British and Americans. 'Life is so isolated now that it is no longer being pollinated by germinating ideas wind-borne from anywhere', was one of *The Bell*'s milder strictures on the national condition. It was a view that has stubbornly resisted modification ever since.

'In every corner of Irish life', wrote the editor of *TCD*, Bethel Solomons Jnr, in 1940, 'a torpid apathy towards the part that we are playing, although it is from the outside, is the only mood existent. The cardinal feature in the life of the average Irishman, even in these times, is happiness to the exclusion of everything else, and it is an indolent type of happiness . . .' 'There was nothing, really, in the condition of neutrality that militated against human happiness', John Ryan was to confirm: 'The goodness of simple things was emphasised rather than diminished by the absence of superfluous luxuries. The country was clean, uncluttered and unhurried. There was no tourism. We could not travel abroad nor could the world come to view us.' But in intellectual circles the native inferiority complex was hard at work, allied to what many felt as a vague sense of guilt. A period, which in theory, should have strengthened the nation by throwing it back on its own resources, spiritual as well as material, was regarded not so much as an opportunity as a sentence of solitary confinement, it being tacitly assumed, that, in spite of the perennial search for new talent (the oft-repeated cry: 'Where are our Young Writers?') no such talent could possibly manifest itself, having been maimed at birth by a deficiency of germinating ideas from 'anywhere'. Few people had any fault to find with this comfortable nihilism, even if they could scarcely have been expected, without the benefit of hindsight, to recognise the talent in their midst. The first number of *The Bell*, for example, carried contributions by, amongst others, Elizabeth Bowen, Patrick Kavanagh, Gerard Murphy, Brinsley MacNamara, Flann O'Brien, Frank O'Connor, Peadar O'Donnell, Seán O Faoláin, Ernie O'Malley, Lennox Robinson, Maurice Walsh and Jack B. Yeats—scarcely a lineup of nonentities. During the Emergency period Kavanagh published *The Great Hunger*, O'Rahilly his seminal theory on the two Saint Patricks, Flann O'Brien *An Béal Bocht*. 'The great tragedy of modern Ireland', lectured *The Bell*, 'is its stifled talent. We know better than most what little leadership there is and how it is trampled on and despised.'

It is arguable what kind of leadership is demanded to achieve the unstifling of stifled talent. To Seán O Faoláin the general atmosphere of cultural philistinism militated against the creative artist; censorship and its attendant evils was a symptom rather than a cause. When James Joyce died in another neutral country, Switzerland, in 1941, the *Irish Independent* described him as having 'reviled the religion in which he had been brought up and fouled the nest which was his native city'. It was a view which would have been supported by a large element of the population, an element which saw nothing strange in the same newspaper's removing the exposed portions of the female figure from its corset advertisements so as to leave two curiously disembodied garments floating in space. In February 1944 the Lenten Regulations of the Archbishop of Dublin, Dr J. C. McQuaid, announced the closing of Trinity College to all Catholics resident within the Dublin diocese. A book by Eric Cross recounting the conversation and opinions of a West Cork couple, *The Tailor and Anstey*, was banned as being in general tendency indecent and obscene, thereby causing intense unhappiness to its innocent protagonists. In October 1943 the management of the town cinema in Clones, Co. Monaghan did their own little bit for morality: 'If you bring a girl friend to the pictures at Clones', reported *The Irish Times*, 'you must sit on one side of the hall and the girl on the other ... Since the beginning of the week these regulations have been rigidly enforced. Married couples are exempt from this rule.' High stepping patrons are encouraged, suggested *Passing Variety*, to avoid tripping over hands clasped across the gangway.

The latter example was simply the lunatic aspect of what was certainly a self-consciously puritanical society, a trend reinforced perhaps by a sense of isolation but by no means created by the condition of neutrality itself. It can be seen, indeed, as an

# TWO GERMAN 'PLANES SHOT DOWN

## —SHIPS ATTACKED

# IRISH TIMES

FRIDAY, FEBRUARY 23, 1940

1. O'Connell Street, Dublin: full on top.

2. Captain Frank Daly (right), of the 26th Infantry Batallion
at Amiens St. Station, Dublin.

3. Phoenix Park pyramid: stock-piling hand-won turf.

4. No standing on the air-raid shelters: Dublin parade, 1942.

24

5. The Palace Guard: Alec Newman, leader writer of the *Irish Times*, gives his editor, R. M. Smyllie, pause for thought. The silent listener on Smyllie's right is M. J. MacManus of the *Irish Press*. The Palace Bar was the visible centre of Dublin literary life.

6. They shall not pass—whoever they are: De Valera, Aiken
(fourth from left) and colleagues review coastal defences.

7   8

9   10

7. On His Majesty's Service: Sir John and Lady Maffey.
8. Seán Lemass, Minister for Supplies.
9. Seán MacBride.
10. Oscar Traynor, Minister for Defence.

attempt, however misapplied, to conserve standards that were being trampled elsewhere, and, though it may have caused some books to remain unwritten, it also gave to many developing talents the opportunity of tilting at domestic windmills of satisfying substantiality.

Isolation from the outside world, if not an entire disaster from the creative point of view, certainly brought certain practical disadvantages in its train. 'The English market has been virtually closed to Irish writers', observed *The Bell* in December 1941; 'The American market has disappeared. This is partly an economic result of the war, but it is largely due also to political reasons. Irish writers, like Irish taxpayers, have to pay for neutrality and for their loyalty to the Government of their own country.' Dependence upon British and American publishers had become firmly established with the virtual disappearance of the native publishing industry in the 'thirties. In 1941 Seán O Faoláin looked through the window of a bookshop and saw three or four Irish books amongst six hundred non-Irish, and it is doubtful even if those four were published in Ireland. He found it humiliating to have to admit that 'for over 30 years, Irish literature has depended on the initiative and enterprise of English and American publishers, and the intelligent interest of English and American readers in Ireland and her affairs.' Humiliating, but also in its own way, stimulating. 'The war has forced on us a cultural self-sufficiency more complete than the most fervant Separatist could have imposed by law', he noted. His own magazine was, perhaps, the most sustained example.

Others had noticed. Edouard Hempel, the German Minister, believed (and he was in a good position to judge) that neutrality had visibly strengthened Irish national self-consciousness. The opposing belligerent could not, in the nature of things, take quite so detached a view. For the British, Ireland's neurality came as a cultural as much as a political shock, and it is against this background that one should, perhaps, interpret the stigmatisations of those critics who could see, and continue to see, in the society of the Emergency period nothing but apathy and unheroic isolation. Ireland became a drop-out from the world, concluded David Thompson, an Englishman who spent the earlier years quietly immured in Co. Roscommon. But it was a drop-out, not so much from the world, as from the British sphere of influence, and it is not surprising that it produced shock waves which manifested themselves in a professed scorn for a hitherto dependable member of the cultural entourage which had suddenly decided, in the cant phrase of a later era, to do its own thing. 'Ireland should take her place', suggested Myles na gCopaleen, 'not among the nations of the earth (who are surely in no position to receive guests at present), but among the dim enigmas of history.' To the British, indeed, Ireland had become an enigma, and an uncomfortable one. 'This country is at the beginning of its creative history, and at the end of its revolutionary history', proclaimed *The Bell*.

A large claim which harboured more than a grain of truth.

But if it was the beginning, it was one which achieved little general recognition at the time. It was one thing to be cognisant of an enforced condition of self-sufficiency, another to profit by it. Earnán de Blagdh, Managing Director of the Abbey Theatre after the death of the poet F. R. Higgins in 1941, appealed in that same year for £200,000 to establish a film industry which would prevent the national individuality of the country from being destroyed. 'We think that this war', *The Irish Times* had cheerfully predicted a few days after its commencement, 'will provide the opportunity for the birth and development of all manner of theatrical talent here at home.' A couple of years later the picture was less rosy, at least in the eyes of Jimmy O'Dea, whose *Gaiety Revels of 1939* ushered in the Emergency.

'What do you imagine to be the effect of the war on the music hall in Ireland?' he was asked.

'You mean the effect of no artists coming across from the other side?'

'That and the chance of new artists coming on the scene.'

'There have been no artists since the war', said Mr O'Dea mournfully; 'We don't breed them.'

*Dublin Opinion*, a couple of years later again, was taking a more optimistic view, as was admittedly its wont. 'Possibly as a curious side consequence of the European war, the theatres in this neutral country have been having the times of their lives. Opportunity has knocked and everyone has heard it.' The Army was inclined to agree. 'Who is the Irish soldier's favourite pin-up girl?' inquired a columnist in one of its journals. 'Among Irish stars of stage and screen there is a galaxy to choose from. Has Ireland not, as her loveliest singer and loveliest looker, May Devitt? Among our actresses shine in Spanish dark beauty Ginette Waddell of the Gate and Lord Longford's starlet, Peggy Mulhall ... Six feet tall, husky-voiced, Breeda *Hello Wonderful* Garvey is one of our most statuesque show girls. Round, chubbily-dimpled artiste Joan Reddin is rightly popular. But maybe you prefer Dame Noel Purcell, all the lean, eight-feet-something length of Dublin cheek of him?'

Maybe they did. There was a ready audience for humour. The country supported two regular monthly humorous journals, and in his introduction to the younger of the two, which began life as *Barrack Variety*, the Minister for Defence, Oscar Traynor, claimed that Irish wit and humour, which he described as the chief antagonist of gloom, abounded probably to a greater degree in the Army than in any other section of the community. A curious claim, in the circumstances, but one which serves to underline the pervading unreality of the situation even in 1942.

The wit and humour, though in plentiful supply, was in general simple and unsophisticated, even by the fairly undemanding standards of the day. Ireland had need of a satirist, and the need was generously if eclectically supplied by Brian

O'Nolan, alias Flann O'Brien, who, under his third, and perhaps most effulgent alias of Myles na gCopaleen, first started appearing in *The Irish Times* on 4 October 1940. W. J. White, who joined the editorial staff in 1942, recalls that, even though the paper was then restricted to four pages a day, *Cruiskeen Lawn* retained its half-column in the leader page. 'By now' he said, 'it had become one of the most prized features of the newspaper, and its author a celebrity.' An anthology was published in 1943. It must be remembered, however, that the circulation of *The Irish Times* was less than 30,000, and largely restricted to the Dublin area and to well-defined levels of society. Though Myles had a play, *Faustus Kelly*, produced in the Abbey on 25 January 1943 (the cast included F. J. McCormick, Denis O'Dea and Cyril Cusack — it ran until early March) and another one, *Thirst*, produced by a young army officer, Alan Simpson, in Mullingar, he could scarcely be described at the time as a national figure. Nevertheless, his relentless sending-up of some of the most sacred institutions and locutions of the period blew like a breath of malt-laden air through the aseptic confines of the Emergency establishment. In the cultural field in particular his aim was deadly. When the Municipal Gallery distinguished itself by refusing to hang a picture by Rouault, he delivered a typically *ex cathedra* judgement: 'The picture was bought for £400 by the Friends of the National Collections and offered as a gift to the Municipal Gallery. (Here let me digress to reiterate once more my demand that the narrow thoroughfare in Parnell Square where the gallery stands should be renamed Hugh Lane.) The Board of the Gallery, presumably composed of members of the Corporation, rejected the picture. The ex-Lord Mayor, Mrs Clarke, is quoted as having said that the picture is a "travesty" and "offensive to Christian sentiments". Mr Keating says it is "childish, naïve and unintelligible" . . .

'The picture is executed in the modern manner, and could not be expected to please persons whose knowledge of sacred art is derived from the shiny chromo-lithograph bon-dieuiserie of the Boulevard Saint Sulpice, examples of which are to be found in every decent Irishman's bedroom. Such persons, however, never enter picture galleries, and there is no obvious reason why their opinion should be considered at all . . .'

In September 1942 a column appeared for the first time in *Barrack Variety* entitled *An Cruiskeen Follamh. By Furlong na nAsailín*. Though only trotting after its acerbic model, it provided some indication of the widening of his influence.

The banning of a single painting was perhaps not a very serious matter (the Rouault was subsequently hung in St Patrick's College, Maynooth); in its broader aspects, however, censorship affected almost every aspect of Emergency life. *Old Moore's*

*Almanac* was seized and censored because, in the words of Frank Aiken, 'it contained matter which would be likely to cause offence to the peoples of friendly nations'. The Presbyterians in Dun Laoghaire were forbidden to insert notices of their services in the newspapers headed 'Kingstown Church, Dun Laoghaire'—presumably they were suspected of a belated gesture of loyalty to the late King George IV of England. 'There is no truth in the rumour that a gentleman has been seen in the corridors of RE (Radio Eireann) armed with a spray and searching for jitterbugs', a humorist commented in March 1944. There was a certain amount of truth in the rumour; the Minister for Posts and Telegraphs, Patrick Little, was an enthusiast for classical music and held a marked antipathy to swing and crooning, which were, in effect, banned from the ether. Radio Eireann suffered from official censorship in other ways; sports commentators, at a loss for the picturesque phrase whilst first aid was being administered on the field of play, were forbidden to allude to the weather even in the most general terms; ecclesiastical authorities, following the utterance from a pulpit of markedly non-neutral opinion, were requested to submit texts of sermons to be broadcast for scrutiny, a request they steadfastly refused. News bulletins, before transmission, had to be read over to the head of the Government Information Bureau. Programmes were also restricted through the need to conserve electricity and the synchronising of the three wavelengths (Dublin, Cork and Athlone) on 530 metres as a security measure. In spite of this, and in the face of almost derisory fees paid to contributors (Jimmy O'Dea and Harry O'Donovan were offered £10 for a broadcast of their pantomime *Hansel and Gretel*) a service was provided which, if failing to satisfy those for whom the BBC could do no wrong, made the most of the available talent. Some of this was outstanding by any standards; both Frank O'Connor and Seán O Faoláin became regular contributors, and the Symphony orchestra, under Vincent O'Brien and later Michael Bowles, attracted a huge following for its public concerts which were inaugurated in 1941 in Dublin's Mansion House and transferred to the Capitol Theatre in 1943, a year which also saw the establishment of Cor Radio Eireann on a part-time basis. Popular programmes such as Question Time and Information Please had a large following, but the number of radio licences fell steadily from the late 1939 figure of 166,275 (1 in 17 of the population) owing to an increasing scarcity of high-tension batteries. Even the offer of the curiously-named 'Vibrator Sets', which operated on low tension batteries only and were described as being 'the ideal receiver for today' failed to solve the problem.

The cinema also had its problems. 'There is a simple moral code, and there are principles on which civilisation and family life are based', said the Film Censor, Richard Hayes, who had succeeded James Montgomery in 1940 ('We had films before our eyes, now we have a Hayes', commented *Dublin Opinion*). 'Any ignoring of these', he went on, 'or any defiance of them in a picture bans it straightaway as far as I am concerned.' There often wasn't much left. During June 1942 you could pay 1s 8d (9p) in the Balcony of the Savoy Cinema, Kilkenny for a feast of the following: *Mr & Mrs Smith*; *A Woman's Face*; *Penny Serenade*; *Nice Girl*; *Night at Earl Carroll's*; *Sun Valley Serenade*; *Tragedy of Divorce*. The stalls at 1s (5p) or the Parterre at 4d (1¼p) might have been considered an adequate outlay in some cases.

It was not only faith and morals, however, that had to be jealously guarded; the censorship regulations required that neither belligerent be favoured in the presentation of war news, which in effect meant a complete ban on overt war films and the meticulous dissection of many others. 'A full ninety per cent of the films we get from England and America these days have more than their fair share of propaganda', the Film Censor complained in 1941: 'and it's the devil's own job cutting it out.' Of Chaplin's *The Great Dictator* he said: 'If that picture had been shown in this country it would have meant riots and bloodshed.' 1,661 films were presented to the Censor in 1942. 362 were passed with cuts and 82 rejected. 52 of the latter were suppressed under the relevant Emergency Powers Orders.

If it was difficult for Dr Hayes it was well-nigh impossible for the newspaper editors, most of whom were disinclined to accept the rulings of the censors without question. Joseph Connolly, formerly of the Board of Works and a close friend of the Minister for the Co-Ordination of Defensive Measures, Frank Aiken, was appointed with his two colleagues, Mike Knightly, a newspaperman, and T. J. Coyne, of the Department of Justice, on Wednesday 6 September 1939. Their severest and most constant critic was R. M. Symllie, editor of *The Irish Times*. 'It is damnably difficult for a newspaper man to cope with our friends in the Castle', he wrote to General Richard Mulcahy, 'it must be equally difficult for public representatives who have the moral courage to be critical. I have bitter experience of the whole hierarchy of Censors. I have found Knightly reasonable, even sympathetic, Coyne casuistically helpful, Joe Connolly a bitter Anglophobe and Aiken unintelligently impossible! Whenever I have appealed to Caesar (and I have done so more than once) I have found the Long Fellow more than anxious to be fair.' (The reference is, of course, to de Valera). The policies of *The Irish Times* were, in any case, almost bound to lead them into conflict with the establishment. 'Our policy is to advocate the maintenance of a strong Commonwealth connection', said Smyllie, 'while insisting, no less strongly, on Irish political independence. In other words, we are in many ways the only real Sinn Féin paper in existence.' But his fundamental objections to censorship was basically more practical. 'My main objection', he said, 'boils down to the fact that Civil Servants know nothing of newspaper work (they lack a sense of humour— that's in the nature of their job) and that, in the end, Censorship tends to defeat its own purpose. For once the public knows that Censorship exists they begin to lose confidence in everything they read.'

There was nothing much that could be done about broadcasts emanating from outside the state (Lord Haw Haw, William Joyce, would have topped present-day TAM-ratings and often exhibited uncanny knowledge of Irish conditions), and there was no ban on British or American papers (including the propagandist *Letter from America*) from entering the country. These, however, were irregular and uncertain in their appearance. 'Up to the present war, the Press in Ireland suffered severely from English competition and it was getting worse every year' said Smyllie, 'but luckily, the war has changed all that. Transport difficulties have made it impossible for Dubliners to have English newspapers on their breakfast-tables.' Quite apart from censorship, however, Irish papers were still at a disadvantage. 'One of our greatest omissions in this war,' said Seán O Faoláin, 'is that our newspapers have no Foreign Correspondents. Here we are in the presence of one of the greatest events of history and no pressmen have been sent to report the match.'

Matches of more local kind, containing little that was explicitly political or sexual, continued to be fully reported, notably by Micheál O'Hehir and a promising young boxer called Éamonn Andrews. Apart from the abandonment of international fixtures and the curtailment of some others due to transport and other difficulties, sporting activities were little affected. Among the influx of refugees from Britain in the early days were a number of well-connected racehorses and their equally well-connected owners and trainers, and race-meetings continued to be held, though finding a method of transporting oneself to them was another matter and one which raised cries of discrimination. In June 1941 the Munster Council of the GAA protested against the GSR's refusal to run special trains to Gaelic fixtures whilst continuing to supply them for the Curragh, Mallow and other race meetings. In other sports some outstanding figures were undoubtedly denied the opportunity of achieving wider fame as a result of the curtailment of international fixtures. Harry Bradshaw won the Native Professional Golf Championship four times in a row, 1941–44; John Burke won the South of Ireland Amateur Open every year from 1941–46; other outstanding golfers were Jimmy Bruen, Cecil Ewing and Joe Carr, several of whom were able to realise their full potential in the post-Emergency era. But in spite of transport and all other difficulties 79,245 people attended the all-Ireland football final between Cavan and Kildare in 1944—a figure which was not to be exceeded until 1953. On 11 June in the same year the Coast Defence Artillery XI had beaten Drogheda United to win the Junior Cup, the first and, at the time of writing, the only such success by an army soccer team.


Wee Beauty, the World's Smallest Pony, arrived in Cork on 8 March 1944 accompanied by a piebald monkey named 'Cherry' and a three-legged hen. Other exhibitions were of a more conventional nature, if not always accepted as such by the public. 'Dublin has been lucky during the last few years in being the scene of heated controversies on certain manifestations of modern painting', suggested a critic in 1944. Apart from the case of the Rouault painting, there had been an exhibition of subjective art in the previous January at the White Stag Gallery in Baggot Street, Dublin; a Continental Painting exhibition, violently attacked by Patrick Kavanagh in the newspapers ('I know nothing about painting but I do know that with the exception of four pictures the rest of the exhibits should be at the bottom of the Liffey') and, in what must rank as an *annus mirabilis*, the first Irish Living Art Exhibition.

'Five years ago', wrote Margot Moffett in the British review *Horizon* in April 1945, 'Eire locked up her artists and increased her export of graduates, technicians and unskilled labour. Here in Dublin in day-to-day life the effect on the community of this export of minds and hands trained to serve the common bondages of England and Eire has not been so evident as the effect of the locking up process of the local artists and new imports.' Others remained unconvinced. The playwright Lennox Robinson complained that artists, in spite of world-shaking events around them continued to paint vases of flowers and nudes on sofas and the blue mountains of the west. Nor did the critics escape. Charles Sydney, in *The Bell*, complained that he had found so many instances of uninformed, irrelevant and misleading writing on the subject of art that it made him wonder how such a state of affairs could have arisen, whilst a future director of the National Gallery, James White, wrote in *The Standard*: 'In this country, unfortunately, criticism has neither the authority which is its first requirement, nor the grace which would keep it in harmony with our other branches of literature. This is largely due to the fact that art criticism appears anonymously in most of our papers.' A state of affairs exemplified, perhaps, by an anonymous comment on one of the few new stamps issued during the period, in this case in honour of the mathematician Sir William Rowan Hamilton:

*'Who's that they have on the new stamp'?*

*'Some fella who discovered a quarter o' onions, or somethin'.'*

"How often do I have to be refused to become a regular customer?"

# Interlude: the usual Three Nuns

*Will our bread supplies last until harvest? If everyone goes easy on bread; if everyone cuts down on wastage; if housewives are careful to make full use of all crusts, cold potatoes, leftover porridge, etc.—if we do these things, there will be no real shortage ...*

Government Notice, June 1941

*The brother has it all worked out ... how we can get through the war here in the Free State. I mean the rationing and brown bread and all that class of thing ... we all go to bed for a week every month.*

MYLES NA GCOPALEEN

HAD THERE been no Emergency, Ireland in the early '40s would scarcely have rated as a gastronome's paradise. The daily diet, for those who could afford it, was solidly conservative; an advertisement suggesting 'a box of Galtee Cheese Sections on the Christmas Table—the perfect ending to a perfect meal' (1941) was daringly innovative. A century before, the Famine had demonstrated that the Irish, in common with other unsophisticated communities, preferred to starve rather than venture upon unfamiliar forms of nourishment, and the same phenomenon was observed and reported upon as the stringencies of the Emergency food situation began to make themselves felt. 'Anyone would think that a neutral island would at least have a supply of fish; but there was none inland and never had been in my time', wrote David Thompson, 'except now and then some uneatable salted pieces: no fresh fish at all even on Fridays for rich or poor . . . no one liked fish. They thought it poor stuff fit only for fasting on.'

'There is nobody in this country who is not getting proper food', Mr de Valera told the people of Kilrush, Co. Clare, in June 1943. But Thompson, from his rural vantage point in Roscommon, saw a different picture. The restrictions in supplies of basic foodstuffs, though causing some discomfort among the middle classes, hit the poor hard, reducing them 'to a level of subsistence as low as the oldest could remember. The shortage of bread was the worst for them, especially in the summer months.' Most of the poor were poor because there were no jobs for them. The 1937 Constitution had proclaimed that the State 'shall in particular, direct its policy towards securing that the citizens . . . may through their occupations find the means of making reasonable provision for their domestic needs', but in 1943 there were 70,000 unemployed, 'as a result of which', commented *The Church of Ireland Gazette* 'malnutrition, destitution disease and crime are widespread'. A year earlier, *The Bell* had levelled a similar charge: 'Malnutrition is prevalent all over the country with its attendant lowering of resistance to disease. Diarrhoea raised the rate of infant mortality alarmingly last summer and T.B. is on the increase. Soon we will have scurvy, rickets, and kindred diseases because we are unable to get a properly balanced diet. Citrus fruits, with their essential Vitamin C, are unobtainable; milk and eggs are dear; tea and sugar are rationed; fish is prohibitive; butter a luxury only the rich can afford; bacon is two shillings (10p) a pound; yet some Bishops expect a starving people to fast *and* abstain . . . a people whose daily diet is little better than a Black Fast every day of the week.'

This degrading picture may or may not have been exaggerated (scurvy, at least, never became a major problem), but it is at least open to question whether the entire blame can be laid upon conditions brought about by the Emergency. Shortages and rationing and the consequent black market certainly, however, accentuated the very wide gap between rich and poor. Seán Mac Thomáis was sent by 'the lady in the big house' to a shop in Dublin's Coombe which sold black market tea at £1 a pound (the normal price was around 15p). 'She always', he said, 'gave me 6d (2½p) for myself.' But with those with the means to support a normal existence there was always food— and drink—to be had, if not always in the quantity and variety that they might have desired. There were very serious shortages of certain commodities: 'When present stocks become exhausted there will be no more cocoa until after the war', Mr Lemass, Minister for Supplies, announced on 17 June 1941. Three days later Dáil deputies from all sides of the House cheered when the Minister announced that the first cargo of wheat purchased in America and shipped to Lisbon in American vessels had arrived at an Irish port. Oranges made their last appearance in Dublin in 1942. Some of these shortages were due simply to the hazards of war; others, to a deliberate policy of economic pressure by the British who, in the conditions then prevailing, could exercise almost complete control over Irish overseas trade. This pressure, was of course, designed originally to force the country to abandon neutrality, but it also arose from a natural resentment on the part of the British at having to risk the lives of their seamen carrying supplies to a non-belligerent. 'Since the outbreak of war they have been living in a world of illusion', said Lord Cranborne. 'They thought that their products and their goodwill were essential to Great Britain, and that she could not afford to let them go short, much less to quarrel with them. They therefore sat back and submitted to the delicious process of being spoon-fed. They were confident that, if they became short of any commodity, the British navy would convoy fresh supplies safely into their harbours. They need themselves do nothing ... It can at any rate be claimed of the new policy that it has brought that frame of mind to an end.'

The frame of mind had, in fact, ended a good time before that. Compulsory tillage had been introduced, increasing pre-war acreage by a million. In February 1941 a Scientific Research Bureau was established to counteract possible shortages, and Mr Lemass's policy was to prepare people for the worst, even if the worst never actually happened. In July 1942, under the heading STOCK EXCHANGE NEWS, *Barrack Variety* reported the situation as follows:

'Rubber was elastic, stretching several points beyond the controlled prices. Tea, weak at 35/- a pound. Coal was slack. Gas gained a little, but soon shaded off. ESB hardened outlook. Tobacco was slow despite brisk demand. Rails were stationary.'

The shortage of tobacco ranked with that of tea and bread as one of the most serious afflictions of the time. Two of the best places for giving out cigarettes to all comers were Brendan Hyland, of Suir Road, and Carthy's of Errigal Road, Drimnagh, and people came from all over Dublin to these two shops to queue for their rations on Fridays and Saturdays. Other tobacconists were less obliging, and drew their share of contumely:

'Why is he walking like that?'

'He's got tobacconist's lumbago.'

'Tobacconist's lumbago?'

'Yes, ducking down under the counter for cigarettes for his special customers.'

And even if supplies were available, they were likely to be in the form of unfamiliar and unpalatable brands; or of equally unacceptable pipe tobacco:

'A Bachelor, Craven A Gold Flake, Afton tried the Senior Services provided by shops in Marino, Grand Parade and the Four Squares. He decided to State

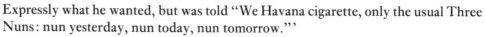

Expressly what he wanted, but was told "We Havana cigarette, only the usual Three Nuns: nun yesterday, nun today, nun tomorrow."'

*Diya know there's a war on?*


A census taken in November 1941 formed the basis of a national register on the evidence of which it was proposed to issue ration books. Mr Lemass was in no hurry: 'The present voluntary system, if we could make it work, will prove to be a much better system than we could operate by means of rationing cards', he told his critics in March 1942, but there were strong pressures on him to introduce rationing and end obvious injustices. Alderman Alfie Byrne, Dublin's recurrent Lord Mayor, got onto his bicycle and made a tour of the tenement quarter which included Waterford Street and Railway Street. He was called over by a very poor woman, Mrs Gleeson of 154 Summerhill. She told him that she had great difficulty in getting bread, showing him one loaf in her arms and telling him: 'That one loaf is for myself and my husband and eleven children.' Ration books were finally brought into use in June 1942, though tea had been allocated by means of a Tea Registration Card since January 1941. This had led to hardships, some retailers refusing, for various reasons, to accept the cards, and there were further hardships when the initial two ounces a week ration was halved and shortly after that halved again. Page G in the ration book (Is page F for butter or worse? it was asked) was for most of the population a sick joke. 'In these days a really good substitute can be made for tea by a mixture of common ash and hawthorn leaves', advised the *Connacht Telegraph* in all seriousness, but most people preferred to distill the last drop of tannin from the conventional product, producing, in a country firm in its allegiance to a strong brew, a liquid of virtually colourless inefficacy. Trotting a mouse (the standard test) across Emergency tea was defined as skating on thin ice. Tea leaves were used several times, and one trick was to put baking powder in the pot, which if achieving nothing else, served to turn the tea leaves white. Tea had traditionally been bought through Britain, but in June 1941 Mr Lemass announced the setting up of a Central Purchasing Company to handle imports direct from the producers. It could do little, however, to bring supplies up to the level of normal requirements. Bread, the other staple of the Irish diet, fared little better. The ending of wheat imports heralded the introduction of the 90 per cent wheat extraction loaf, undoubtedly nourishing but anathema to many Irish palates. 'Won't it be great when normal times return and we can get rid of this fine, healthy energy-giving wholemeal bread and get a couple of slices off a white loaf again?' was the cry in 1943. The white loaf, did, in fact return at the end of that year, leaving in its wake an ingrained prejudice against brown bread which is still reflected in consumption patterns. For putting on bread there was in general plenty of butter, but more sophisticated toppings were less readily available. 'No jars, no jam!', proclaimed one advertiser. 'Please go easy with the Marmite', pleaded another in December, 1941. The pleas became progressively more agonized: 'PLEASE go easy with the Marmite' (January 1942); 'Please spread the Marmite thinly!' (February). Eggs were date-stamped for the protection of customers:

'The number in the ring
Is the most important thing'

advised the Department of Agriculture. 'Increased food production is still of supreme importance', the same ministry was asserting as late as March 1945. 'The future is so uncertain that this country can face it with a feeling of security only if we make ourselves independent of imported food supplies', and it urged everyone to cultivate an allotment. In spite of compulsory tillage and heroic gestures such as the ploughing up of the polo ground in Dublin's Phoenix Park (suspected by some as being more a manifestation of class warfare than of exemplary patriotism) there had been shortages of home grown produce. 'The Murphy family have returned to town after an absence of several weeks' it was announced in June 1943, and though the staple ingredients for the wines of the country were home produced, the preferred potation was not always available in quantities considered adequate to the occasion. One advertiser was moved to caution against excess in the manner of Ogden Nash:

'everyone admits that where whiskey, or for that matter any other drink from water to angostura bitters is concerned, tullamore dew is peerless,
and that without it life would be absolutely cheerless.
so remember this the next time you are drinking it, and don't drink so much that all the tullamore dew is drunk only by a few.
be moderate, restrain yourself, give every man his dew.'

Increases in the price of this particular commodity were greeted with the customary alarm and despondency. 'He's drinking to make himself forget', said the character in the pub. 'What's he trying to forget?' asked his friend. 'The price of drink.' A new Intoxicating Liquor Bill, introduced into the Dáil in 1942, stirred even the most somnolent TDs to flights of rhetoric. They were particularly critical of the proposals to abolish the Bona Fide trade, a convenience for benighted travellers that had, with the increase in mobility, led to flagrant abuse. 'It is well known', said the Minister for Justice, Mr Boland, introducing the second stage of the Bill in October, 'that at the present time people leave licensed premises in the County Borough and take a car or a bus out into one of those areas where this bona fide traffic is permitted, and remain drinking on licensed premises there until the small hours of the morning. This thing has become a gross public scandal.' His proposal to abolish the bona fide system altogether was finally amended in favour of a curtailment which was nevertheless rigorous enough to dismay serious drinkers. Myles na gCopaleen, with the interests of the latter at heart, suggested that public houses should be permitted to open only between two and five in the morning. 'This means that if you are a drinking man you'll have to be in earnest about it', he warned.

In the meantime, there was a steady movement of both food and drink out of the country. A threat to cut off Guinness supplies to Britain in response to that country's intransigence was taken very seriously, particularly in Northern Ireland, but the outflow of other products was in general affected only by belligerent action or commercial considerations. Foodstuffs included canned rabbit ('My bunny flies over the ocean'), as well as more conventional canned meat. Between 25 and 30 million pounds of the latter were produced in 1942, most of it for export to Britain. Furlong na nAsailín saw great possibilities in the canning industry as a whole:

> 'California cans fruit
> Clover cans meat
> The Aga Khan's horses
> Louis Quinze chairs
> Guiness cans men.'

But the British were not always quite so enthusiastic. From midnight on 30 November 1941 they banned imports of Irish pressed meat following several reports on the unsatisfactory condition of shipments. Meat on the hoof was not affected though farmers continued to grumble about the poor prices being paid for fat cattle and stores. There was talk from time to time of attempts to interest the British in a barter system. On ascertaining that domestic whiskey stocks were adequate for the forseeable future, the Cavan TD Patrick Smith asked Mr Lemass to consider bartering three years' supply for extra petrol and coal. The Minister for Supplies was not impressed.

Clothes rationing was at first stigmatised as unnecessary; there were ample supplies in the country and, what was worse, people were cancelling orders already placed when coupons were demanded. There were also complaints about the number of coupons exacted for workers' overalls. There was some panic buying. Myles na gCopaleen knew a man who got wind that cloves were going to be rationed. 'He was cute and set about buying every vestige of this commodity that was on offer ... He got a nice let-down, with parsley on it, when he learnt later that it was clothes—not cloves—that people had been talking about.' And this from the agony column: 'WOMAN who bought 3 pairs black court shoes size 4 (misfit) on 13 June 1942 would exchange for small quantity tinned food'. It was clear, however, that the country was to be reduced to 'an island of scants and collars', and left with barely a belt to tighten. The female section of the population found itself the hardest hit. 'Though pure silk stockings are unobtainable we are still left with artificial silk, though at prices as high as we formerly paid for pure silk', complained Eileen O'Faoláin. 'And so we weary ourselves going from shop to shop trying to get a fully-fashioned artificial stocking at a price which our purses will allow'. For the lazy, Afton Cigarette Coupons offered a pair of Ladies' Silk Hose (one ration coupon) for 175 Coupons. For the lazier still, stockings could be painted on. 'I hate snow, it always washes off my stockings', a sufferer complained in the hard winter of 1944–45. The future, as far as hosiery was concerned, was bleak. 'The whisper is nylon', Eileen O'Faoláin confided, 'but in the opinion of those to whom I have spoken it will never replace silk.'

Another unrealised portent was contained in the suggestion that the new utility men's suits with fewer pockets would give an opportunity to designers of gent's natty handbags, but speculation reached perhaps its liveliest level with the newspaper announcement, under the heading WOMEN'S GARMENTS TO GO, that 'at least ten women's garments will disappear shortly for the duration of the emergency if they are, in the opinion of the Government, "unnecessary during wartime" and if they are made of material which could be used for more essential clothing.' The report suggested that evening gowns would probably be the first casualty, adding that 'there is no indication, as yet, as to what the other garments will be'.

Apart from those who couldn't afford to utilise their full ration anyway, some were harder hit than others. The serving soldier was allotted, theoretically, the same number of coupons as the civilian, but the army promptly cancelled those they estimated would be needed to allow him the uniform he wore. What was left would not even get him a shirt for off-duty wear. For those still with coupons, determining the best way to dispose of them presented some problems: a three-piece gent's suit demanded forty, as against seventeen for a nightshirt and eighteen for a kilt.

Other shortages (and the shopkeeper's handy phrase 'They're not making them any more' covered a wide range of articles and accessories) were of more limited impact. The paper shortage caused the Irish Industrial Waste Co. to advise the public, admittedly in its own interests, that 'anyone who negligibly (sic) uses old newspapers, magazines, torn books, etc. for lighting fires is helping to create unemployment in the printing industry.' Unemployment in *The Irish Times* was averted in July 1942 by the delivery of 10 tons of newsprint from its rival and confirmed political antagonist, the *Irish Press*. And it was suggested that special cheap editions of novels for women readers could be printed, containing only the beginning and the end.

Restrictions in supplies inevitably led to increases in prices, both official and black market, and the scarcity of goods was equalled in most sections of the community by the deficiency in the wherewithal to buy them. Mr James Dillon complained in November 1941 that he had been scouring the country for pence and halfpence and that the banks had told him that they could not get any. It was a not uncommon predicament.

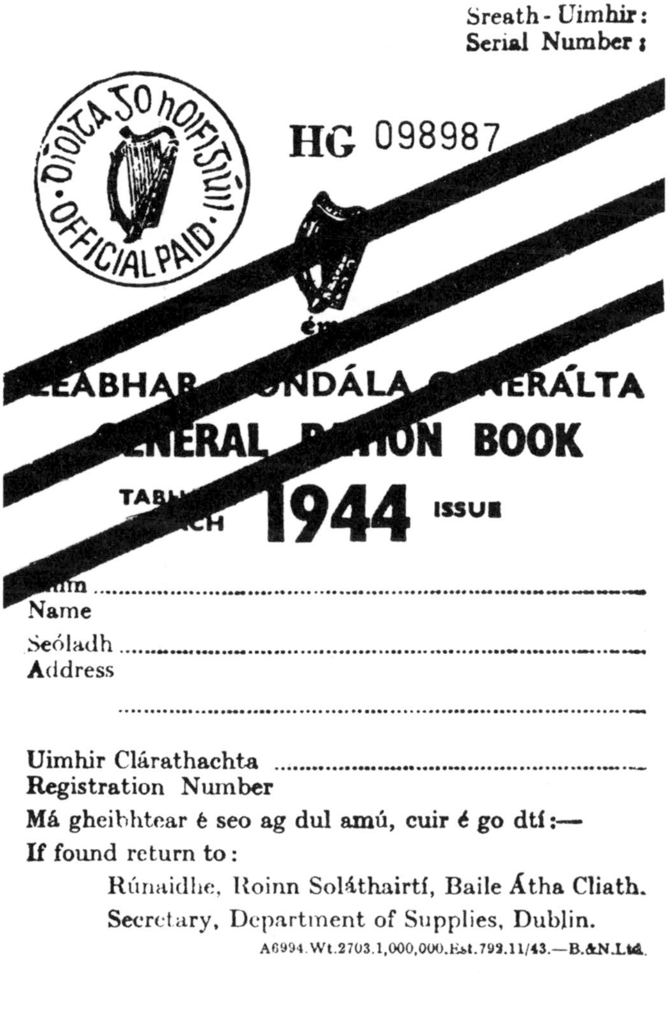

Sreath - Uimhir:
Serial Number:

HG 098987

LEABHAR RONDÁLA GENERÁLTA

GENERAL RATION BOOK

1944 ISSUE

Name

Seóladh
Address

Uimhir Clárathachta
Registration Number
Má gheibhtear é seo ag dul amú, cuir é go dtí:—
If found return to:
Rúnaidhe, Roinn Soláthairtí, Baile Átha Cliath.
Secretary, Department of Supplies, Dublin.
A6994.Wt.2703.1,000,000.Est.799.11/43.—B.&N.Ltd.

# The pillars of independence

*Thomas Davis, a century ago, looking forward to a future Ireland in national health, spoke of the time when 'every young man would be trained, and every grown man able to defend her coast, her plains, her towns, and her hills—not with his right arm merely, but by his disciplined habits and military accomplishments. 'These', said Davis, 'are the pillars of independence'.*

EAMON DE VALERA, 1941

*If only he would come out of the clouds and quit talking about the quarter of a million Irishmen ready to fight if they had the weapons, we would all have a higher regard for him. Personally I do not believe there are more than one thousand trained soldiers in the whole of the Free State ...*

FRANKLIN D. ROOSEVELT, 1942

IRELAND entered the Emergency period with 630 officers, 1,412 NCOs and 5,452 privates. In the A and B Reserve there were 194 officers, 544 NCOs and 4,328 privates. The addition of the Volunteers (237 officers, 557 NCOs and 6,429 privates) brought the total strength up to just under 20,000. These forces were fully mobilised in the early days of September. The maximum strength of the army never rose beyond two divisions and two independent brigades. In the battle for the Low Countries in May 1940 the Germans disposed of 136 divisions.

In the month following the German invasion of Holland and Belgium the Government formally declared a State of Emergency and created the category of Emergency Durationist, or E-man, who would be permitted to enlist for the duration of the Emergency and who rapidly came to outnumber the regular and reserve forces. In 1942, the year which saw large-scale manoeuvres on the Blackwater, the total strength was 38,787 all ranks. A civilian 'war correspondent' covering that event was impressed when he saw a party of Army engineers struggling in the river with planks and scaffolding: 'it was then that it struck me that the spirit of this Army of ours was really so amazingly impervious to the everyday inconveniences of the soldier's life. A little thing, you will say, a little thing for soldiers to stand stripped to the waist in midstream, played with by an autumn breeze, when thousands of their profession all over the world are undergoing so many tortures in various climes. Aye, a little thing perhaps, but it was the spirit in which the officers and men accepted the task that struck me so much . . .' 'A happy army', the Minister for Defence, Oscar Traynor, had said earlier in the same year, 'is one which sees the light and the dark side of its existence and is prepared to treat either of these with that youthful abandon which laughs at all obstacles, grave and gay.'

The members of Oglaigh na hEireann, both temporary and permanent, were of course aware of the existence of other armies in which youthful abandon was perhaps less highly regarded. In the Summer of 1940 in K. Lines in the Curragh Camp (5th Brigade, 3rd, 16th and 25th Battalions) every second soldier had been in Dunkirk, or claimed that he had. 'Morale was good', recalled a member of the 3rd Battalion of a later period, 'and those few desertions that had taken place were occasioned by letters from brothers and pals telling of rapid promotions available to trained Irish soldiers in the British forces. It wasn't so much a gesture of turning one's back on the mother country that caused deserters to slip across the border but a desire to put to the real test all they had been trained for at home.' Other assessments were less charitable. Oliver Flanagan TD offered to furnish the Minister for Defence with the names of certain high officers in the Army who, he said, had made representations to the British Government to get their sons into that country's army as cadets. When the Irish Army is good enough for their fathers, he protested, why is it not good enough for the sons? There were vestiges, too, of identity problems. Brian Inglis, late of *The Irish Times* and on leave from an RAF camp in Northern Ireland, used to meet Irish army officers from Finner Camp in the hotel bar in Bundoran. 'A few of them were from Anglo-Irish families; men who had made up their minds that as their homes and families were in Ireland they should offer their services to their own country's defence. For anybody in our set it needed courage to make this decision. The 'Free State Army', as we still thought of it, had won some reputation for its equestrian capabilities at the horse show, but otherwise none of us took it seriously.' Inglis's attitude rapidly changed, along with most of those who came into contact with the Army of the Emergency. But its abilities had yet to be put to the test.

And no one knew when or from what direction the real test would come—if it came. Rumours of invasion were constant, and on at least one occasion, according to General Richard Mulcahy, the whole army was placed on a fighting footing and General Absolution given in several barracks. This was in December 1940, when the putative invader was the British army, from bases in Northern Ireland. At a conference with the Chief of Staff in the following April the General and his Fine Gael colleagues were shown a line of defence which it was hoped to hold, again against the British, for two months. It may or may not have been optimistic. Certainly the Army was under no illusions about its ability to repel an invasion, from whatever quarter, unaided. Quite apart from the question of manpower and training, equipment was sadly lacking. Negotiations for the setting up of a small arms factory had been in progress and had reached an advanced stage when they were nullified by the outbreak of war in Europe; and the Ordnance Corps were obliged to improvise. An advance of £2000—disapproved of by civil servants who preferred the formalities of competitive tender—was made to the Great Southern Railway Co. to begin production of the no. 36 HE Grenade at their Inchicore works. The GSR succeeded in casting bodies, strikers and centrepieces but S.E. Holmes of Monasterevan was asked to produce the base and filler plugs and Messrs Hilton the springs, whilst the anvils were pressure die-cast in a special zinc alloy by the Jewellery and Metal Manufacturing Co., Kevin Street, Dublin on machines normally employed, appropriately enough, for producing coffin fittings. The completed grenades were filled by military personnel at the Magazine Fort in the Phoenix Park, Dublin, the scene of the army's first major Emergency operation.

Christmas 1939 was seasonably but untypically snowy in the Dublin area. Most Army personnel who could make the journey had gone home for the holiday, when units of the IRA staged a spectacular raid on the Magazine Fort and escaped with large quantities of weapons and ammunition. An announcement was immediately broadcast ordering all ranks back to their stations by the quickest possible means. As soon as they reached their depots the men were organised into lorryloads and sent to the Dublin areas, where, under the direction of the Chief of Staff, Major General Michael Brennan, they were deployed in cordons and search-parties, an operation which continued in severe winter conditions for ten days and nights. In the end more arms and ammunition were found than had been stolen, but the incident left a stigma in spite of the Army's efficient handling of the recovery operations. More than two years later General Mulcahy noted in a memo he made of the Defence Conference at 2 February 1942: 'Traynor explained that some of the old Garrison of the Fort had been selling old ammunition probably to be distributed to the IRA and that the IRA wanted Thompson Gun ammunition. It was suggested to them to come and take it.' Whatever the truth of that assertion, it indicated that a bad taste still lingered.

Most of the Army's difficulties however, were of a more mundane nature. For a start there was an accommodation problem; the existing barracks, most of them inherited from the British regime, were inadequate to house the expanded forces and many derelict and semi-derelict castles in different parts of the country were taken over and restored, if only temporarily, to something of their former vitality. A young officer of the period described the beginning of a normal day in one such establishment: 'I look over the dining hall before the men come in—tables scrubbed white, forms and floors without stain, fire burning and breakfast ready and waiting. The men file past the table for the issue of rations—egg and rasher and a pint of torrid tea as rich and brown as one of Gaugin's Tahitian girls.' (A similar meal was described by an actual partaker thereof as 'a mug of tea, a quarter loaf of bread with a stain of butter, a bit of fatty rasher and a green-white-and-yellow egg'.) The young officer, however, registered no complaints and went off to have his own breakfast. 'I have time to read the communiques of the Powers who are fighting out their private differences before the trumpet blows for "Boots and Saddle" and for my appearance at parade. The parade is formed up in the courtyard of a country house in the midst of a fat and rolling grassland—one troop of a crack Cyclist Squadron engaged in protective and guard duties . . .'

The Cyclist Squadrons were more informally known as 'The Piddling Panzers'. Of equipment appropriate to real Panzer Units there was distressingly little. In September 1939 the Army possessed thirteen Rolls-Royce light armoured cars some twenty years old, each armed with a Vickers .303 machine gun, and twelve Swedish medium armoured cars, together with four of a similar type constructed in Ireland on a Leyland Terrier chassis. Four more were on order from Sweden, but unfortunately were shipped via the Netherlands where they arrived about the same time as the invading German forces. There was no immediate prospect of further supplies from any source, so the Swedish Landsverks were kept operational by means of spares made by S. E. Holmes of Monasterevan, and once again the Great Southern Railway Company was invited to assist. Mr Breedon, who was the Chief Mechanical Engineer at Inchicore, built armoured cars on a Ford chassis, using old steel plate which had been retrieved from Royal Irish Constabulary barracks years before and which was case-hardened and tested for efficacy at Kilbride firing range. The resultant vehicle did not greatly appeal to the Cavalry, and later models were built by Thomas Thompson & Co. of Carlow. By late 1940 there were enough of these unorthodox vehicles available to equip three armoured squadrons and Colonel J. B. Lawless, Director of Cavalry and Commandant A. W. Mayne, who were jointly responsible for the design, subsequently adapted it to a Dodge chassis. The British later supplied some Bren Gun carriers and Beaverettes, but the home-produced armour provided the mainstay of the Cavalry Corps throughout the Emergency period.

If the civilian sector was at times called in to assist the military with specialist services, the converse was also true. The Emergency Scientific Research Bureau set up by the Government had its counterpart in the Army Research and Production Branch, which was under the control of the Director of Ordnance. In early 1941 the firm of Maguire and Patterson found itself short of the necessary materials for the production of matches and asked Research and Production for assistance in the manufacture of phosphorous sesquisulphide and potassium chlorate. The project, when examined, proved to be feasible but too expensive. The army did, however, produce its own phosphorous for use in explosives using phosphate rock, first from Florida and later from Co. Clare (a state company, Comhlucht Lorgtha agus Forbartha Mianrai, handled most of the extraction). The ore was treated in an electric furnace erected in the laundry building at Parkgate, Dublin, where a plant for the production of potassium chlorate also eventually commenced production in 1944, rendering belated but valuable assistance to the match industry.

When the National Blood Transfusion Council was set up in April 1942 it was supervised jointly by Professor R. A. Q. O'Meara of Trinity College, Dublin and Commandant T. Dodd, Pathologist at St Bricin's Military Hospital, where the base laboratory was utilised as the production unit. Army units in the Dublin area supplied the first donors. Among the many essentials then unobtainable was laboratory glassware, and serum was collected and stored in milk bottles which had to be sterilised in the early hours of the morning because of the restriction in gas supplies. The public at large were not directly involved until June 1944, when a premises at 115 Grafton Street became the National Blood Transfusion Centre. It was not, in fact, operative until early the following year, when its success was at least partly accounted for by the fact that it offered donors a cup of tea for their services at a time when the weekly ration stood at half an ounce.

The troops, too, were grateful for small comforts. Whatever about tea à la Gaugin, Army life was hard enough on those with small resources and large appetites. In 1942 a private's pay was 14s (70p) a week, from which was compulsorily deducted 2d ($\frac{1}{2}$p) for a haircut, 6d ($2\frac{1}{2}$p) for laundry and 2d for social welfare. Food, apart from the breakfast menu already described, was, on paper at least, adequate: a daily allowance of '$\frac{3}{4}$ lb of best home fed beef, 1 lb of bread, 14 ozs potatoes, $\frac{1}{4}$ lb of fresh vegetables, $\frac{5}{6}$ pint of fresh milk and a liberal quantity of butter, cheese, jam, eggs, bacon and sausages, along with many other little extras that constitute appetising meals.'

Translated into the daily menu at Portobello Barracks, Dublin, this became typically, Breakfast: Tea, bread and butter, rasher and pudding; Dinner: Brown Stew, Mixed Vegetables, Potatoes, Jam Roll, Tea; Tea: Tea, Bread and Butter, Meat rissoles; Supper: Tea, bread and butter.

The food at Brugh an Airm, O'Connell Street, Dublin, was similar in its unpretentious solidity: a meal consisting of one rasher, two sausages and mashed potatoes could be obtained for a shilling (5p). Brugh an Airm was a hostel set up by the Army Welfare Association, a voluntary organisation, and opened by the Minister for Defence on 21 March 1941. It catered for any 'Oglach Galunach, Seosamh' who might find himself without a bed in the big city and charged 2s 6d (12$\frac{1}{2}$p) for overnight accommodation plus breakfast. Its thirty beds were nearly always fully occupied. Similar clubs (there were recreational as well as sleeping facilities) were subsequently opened in Cork, Limerick and Galway. Another voluntary civilian organisation, the Soldiers' Comforts Fund, was established in 1940 by a group of public-spirited ladies. In 1943 Miss Maureen Joyce won the Knitting Competition with a tally of twelve pairs of socks and thirty-six pullovers, completed in a period of three months.

On a more sartorial level, a new-style uniform was introduced in 1940. (The German-style 'coal scuttle' helmets had also been replaced.) The 'jildy file', or smart soldier, was now a good deal more comfortable and his uniform consisted basically of a brass-buttoned tunic with roll collar, long trousers with ankle straps, and a forage cap which could be opened out in bad weather. The colour was light grey-green, with short leather leggings ('jam pots') and ruby-red leather boots. The total effect, as described by the young officer already quoted, was indeed a vision splendid: 'Hanratty's helmet is sitting straightly, his badges and buttons shining; his equipment "blancoes" and its brasses winking proudly at his buttons; his field slacks so mattress pressed that they might stand up without the support of legs inside them and his boots breaking the pale gleam of the morning into a million little dancing spears of ruby light.' 'Potentially', said the Minister for Defence, Oscar Traynor, 'we are the best soldiers in Europe' . . .

. . . but some difficulty was experienced in achieving that full potential. 'We are not at all anxious to bring in conscription', de Valera told the Dáil in December 1941, 'and I feel that it will not be necessary'. He was reacting to adverse criticism of the recruiting drive to date. The situation had not materially improved by 1943: 'This is not time for slackers or shirkers', Oscar Traynor informed the nation. 'Even if a man is so devoid of national consciousness, so lost to all sense of honour as to shirk taking his part in his country's defences, surely he cannot be foolish enough to have lost interest in his own preservation'. Frank Aiken, Minister for the Co-Ordination of Defensive Measures, put the same idea more modestly: 'Though this old and war-battered country is still very far from being a Utopia, it is worth fighting for. Its survival through this world crisis is well worth a few years hard soldiering by every young man who intends to live in it . . .'

Mullingar, in March 1942, was the first town to stage a *Step Together* week, an event held under the auspices of the Army and combined volunteer services with the aim of stimulating recruiting. According to one witness the troops were led into the town by a fiddler and an accordionist playing *Roll out the Barrel*. Athlone followed suit on 28 June, and the message from Colonel F. McCorley, O/C, Western Command, printed in the official programme, did not mince words. 'It is regrettable', he wrote, 'that, even now, after nearly three years of universal war, it should be found necessary to advertise the fact that the Regular Army, the L.D.F., L.S.F., Red Cross, and kindred Services, are still far short of the numbers required. I know that Athlone and the neighbouring districts have given a response to the appeal for men for the L.D.F. which will compare very favourably with that in any part of the country; nevertheless, even here there are still too many standing idly by.'

But in the face of the invasion that never came it was increasingly difficult to sustain interest sufficient to attract new recruits. In the Army itself similar difficulties were being experienced. 'Last month I told you', Major General Aodh Mac Neill wrote in the Second Division's journal in February 1943, 'we were overhauling our entire system of military training proper. It is a good time to overhaul our system of mental training as well. This is the purpose behind our recently introduced "Wall Newspapers" . . .'

The peak of interest had probably been attained with the great autumn manoeuvres of 1942, in which no effort was spared to achieve maximum realism, even to the imposing of conditions of secrecy on the reporters covering the event. The *Irish Press* man headed his first dispatch, which appeared in the paper on Tuesday 1 September, 'South of Ireland—Monday night', and continued: 'On the eve of the biggest mimic battle ever staged in this country two great armies, equipped with all types of modern armament, face one another in the heart of a fertile valley extending over South Tipperary, part of Waterford and North Cork.

'This beautiful countryside conceals thousands of troops which had been moved up to camouflaged positions on either side of a great river which separates the opposing forces by a substantial interval.

'A very real tenseness pervades the advanced encampments where the troops are keyed up to go into action at the word of command, which may be given at any moment.

'The Army's greatest manoeuvres ever are being taken in deadly earnest. The most strict secrecy about troop movements and other matters of military importance is being observed.

'Though as a Pressman I have been privileged to see much that is going on behind the scenes, I am not allowed to mention any place names nor to describe the area in such a way as to give the slightest idea as to its location.' (Though there is a limit to the number of 'great rivers' in South Tipperary, Waterford and North Cork.)

The manoeuvres, understandably enough, aroused great local interest. 'People in the towns and villages of the Munster "War Zone" stayed up all night to watch the start of the battle between the Red and Blue armies now locked in a tense struggle', the correspondent wrote on the third, adding that they were rewarded for their pains with many thrills. On the following day he watched the opposing forces battling for the possession of 'the big river which runs between their lines'. 'Now three nights without sleep, continuously engaged in herculean tasks in appalling conditions of discomfort, these soldiers of Ireland's Defence Forces startled me by the dash and fury with which they hurled themselves into the major engagement now beginning.'

The soldiers, he wrote the next day, had been taken into the homes and the hearts of the people. On Monday the 7th his news was grimmer: 'Lieutenant T. A. Ryan, Cashel, and Sergeant J. McElligott, Listowel, lost their lives while attempting to cross a river during the Army manoeuvres yesterday'. Two major engagements in the vicinity of the 'big river' were followed by a two-day engagement in which the LDF, the Marine Service and the Maritime Inscription took part, and the week culminated with a parade through Cork city which was the biggest in the country's history to date and at which the Taoiseach took the salute. The Department of Defence was quick to seize an obvious opportunity with an advertisement in the papers the following day:

## THE PEOPLE OF CORK

had the opportunity yesterday of seeing our own Army march past the saluting base in the South Mall, while overhead flew the machines of our Air Corps.

These splendidly trained men, resolutely determined to defend their Motherland, presented an inspiring sight as they marched in Divisions, Brigades, Battalions and Companies. No doubt many men who watched this parade were thrilled at the sight of our Volunteer Army and wished that they too were in the ranks.

There is room for them and they will be welcomed as comrades. All who are free to join should enlist NOW for the duration of the emergency and be trained to give the same grand service as the magnificent men who paraded yesterday.

Invasion always remained a possibility, though an increasingly unlikely one as the tide of war turned elsewhere. 'Government policy as outlined to us is simply this: "Whoever comes first is our enemy",' T. F. O'Higgins had complained to General Mulcahy in 1941, and when James Dillon had suggested to de Valera that the country was likely to find itself in the position in which it was at war with the United States, Great Britain and Germany combined, the Taoiseach had admitted that he had considered such a disastrous eventuality.

In the event, however, none of the awkward questions had to be answered, and to what extent the strength, efficiency and determination of the Army acted as a deterrent to any potential invader remains largely a matter for speculation. Major-General M. J. Costello, General Officer Commanding the First Division, at least left no doubt in the minds of his men as to the value of their contribution in a Special Order addressed to them and dated 10 May 1945: 'This is not a rich country and the Government has done a big and generous thing in making your gratuities so big', he told them: 'Having watched you in training, on manoeuvres, at work on the bogs, or round your Barracks, having seen your exemplary conduct in public towards the civil population, I know you deserve it all. I have said often that your service as soldiers was magnificent. You deserve the very best the country can do for you. But in this life people usually deserve more than they get. For once the reward in your case is equal to your splendid record as soldiers. I confidently rely upon you to be worthy of the generous reward you are getting. This money comes from the tax payers who have had to earn it hard themselves. Some of them might not like to see you getting so much of it.'

For many whose lives had been permanently reshaped by the Call to Arms, the journey back to the reality of peace, however big the gratuity, was to be both painful and disillusioning.

" *Now* I know there's a war on ! All different colours . . . and all the same taste ! "

HOW DUNDALK STATION MUST APPEAR TO NORTHERN VISITORS RETURNING FROM DUBLIN

# Interlude: a shilling a leg to Salthill

*SEE IRELAND FIRST IN SPITE OF THE
EMERGENCY*
*Cruises by Canal Boat*
*FORTNIGHT'S CRUISE for 15 guineas, saloon 20
guineas. One week in Glamorous Kilcock. Dancing on deck
every night. First class cuisine—bacon and cabbage every
day . . . See the native Kilcock boys diving for 'wings' and
'makes'. Dance with the Kilcock girls, District Justice
—— permitting.*

Barrack Variety

*Courteous children always sit
So that three per seat may fit.*

Dublin United Transport Co.

THE EMERGENCY contributed its quota of neologisms; 'bailing out' was one of
them. To most people this meant involuntary departure from an aircraft in
flight; but to the men whose job it was to keep the country's railways operating
it had a somewhat different connotation. Once, when a locomotive foreman
contacted his District Superintendent by telegram with the information that several
drivers had bailed out, the Gardaí, who had intercepted the message, assumed that

the half-expected invasion had finally taken place, headed, presumably, by bogus footplate-men. For drivers on the Great Southern Railways (the Great Northern was another matter) 'bailing out' had become a regular and unwelcome part of the daily routine. It meant cleaning out the fire, sometimes after a journey of only five miles or so, and relighting it with timber from any available source. Driver Martyn White, of the former Dublin South Eastern section, once came upon almost every engine from the Grand Canal Street and Bray depots at a standstill at Dun Laoghaire station. 'I was the last to arrive', he recalled, 'and, like the others, could proceed no further. The Shunter asked me whether I could go around my train and haul it to Salthill out of the way, as the whole station was blocked by stranded engines and coaches. I succeeded, but to my great surprise, when I reached Salthill, there were a lot of passengers on the platform, who boarded my train. I decided to keep going, and hope for the best. On arrival at each station the cry went out for more timber, and timber we got! My last supply was picked up near Sydney Parade station—a number of planks lying beside the line, which we broke up between the spokes of the wheels of our engine'. The papers next morning recorded the fact that a train had taken three hours to travel from Dun Laoghaire to Dublin, a distance of some seven miles.

This was in no way an isolated occurrence. A train from Broadstone Station, Dublin, to Athlone, a route which parallels the Royal Canal, was passed twice by a canal barge whilst bailing out. GSR no. 800, *Maedhbh*, the big 4-6-0 that was the pride of the Great Southern, having been put into service in 1939, was listed as 'missing' for several days, being finally discovered at the back of Mountrath Goods Store, where her exhausted crew had abandoned her after a particularly gruelling bailing-out session. In the winter of 1942 it took a passenger train twenty-three hours to cover the 210 miles from Killarney to Dublin. April of the same year had seen the 'temporary' closure of eleven branch lines (for several of them it was effectively a death sentence) and on all other lines services were cut to two days a week for passenger trains, four for freight. In October of the previous year coal stocks had dwindled to one day's supply, and the Government had been obliged to utilise the emergency dumps in Dublin's Phoenix Park.

Steam locomotives did not take kindly to the available substitutes. Turf was too bulky, of insufficient calorific value, and created insuperable disposal problems, though Myles na gCopaleen suggested that all railway lines should be relaid to traverse the bogs and that locomotives should be fitted with a patent scoop apparatus. Wood was slightly more acceptable but was not available in sufficient quantities. Conversion to oil-burning was, of course, out of the question, so a new fuel, 'duff'—a mixture of dust and pitch—made its unwelcome appearance. 1500 tons per week were being produced by late 1942, but proved a makeshift substitute at best. The Great Southern continued to use anything burnable in its efforts to maintain even skeleton services.

The situation as regards the Great Northern was very different. Serving both sides of the Border, and providing an essential service for troop and supply movements in the North, it was guaranteed a supply of coal by the British authorities that was the envy of the GSR drivers. At Amiens Street, where the two systems converged, it was not unknown for a GSR fireman to 'prig' a supply from a GNR locomotive standing on an adjacent track. But this was the exception; most of the system had to make do with whatever came to hand, and many scheduled services failed to start, or, having started, to arrive. As a porter on a country station was overheard to remark in wonderment to a colleague: 'Here she comes, Tom, right on the day!'

Fuel shortages were exacerbated by deficiencies in equipment and personnel. The third locomotive of the '800' class, the *Tailte*, though virtually complete at the beginning of the Emergency, was not put into service until June 1940. There was a scarcity of goods wagons, and turf was carried from the western and midland bogs to Dublin in old six-wheeled passenger coaches (known with some justification as 'bug boxes') with the roofs removed. A rundown of staff in the depressed conditions of pre-Emergency days had created a shortage of experienced firemen. But in other ways Emergency conditions were a godsend to the ailing railway system. No alternative means of transport was available to the public, and all services, particularly those bringing holiday-makers and steak-hunters from the North, were packed to capacity. In May 1940 the Great Southern was advertising 'A Week in the West 1st Class Rail, 1st Class Hotel £8 18s 9d' (£8.94 approx). In the same month a GNR special train took Dublin newspaper and advertising men to Bundoran for their annual outing, throwing them together, as one participant remembered 'in unusual harmony for a weekend's drinking interrupted only by the competition for the Publicity Challenge Cup'. Bundoran station, thanks to the operation of Double Summer Time in the North, dispatched its first train at the un-Irish hour of 5.30 a.m., and the GNR service which left Derry for Belfast at 7.15 a.m. found itself arriving in St Johnston, Co. Donegal at 6.30 a.m., three-quarters of an hour before it had started.

Such feats were hardly within the compass of the canal traffic, which, shared, though to a more limited extent, in the railways' brief return to universal popularity. Twenty-nine new wooden barges were ordered in 1942 for the vital turf traffic (powered by horses, they could in theory be hired from the Government by anyone with access to the necessary prime mover) and the locks on the Grand Canal were operated on a round-the-clock basis. Less fortunate were the few remaining coastal shipping services—the Bantry Bay Steamship Co., which ran a public service between Castletown, Glengarrif, Adrigole and Bere Island, was threatened with complete closure in mid-1942 through lack of coal and its vessel, the *Princess Beara*, was finally immobilised through lack of fuel and spare parts in 1944. And, since coal was the mainstay of the electricity supply, Dublin's electric trams were curtailed in 1942 and suspended completely for the summer of 1944. They had, in any case, been giving way to buses for reasons not directly connected with the Emergency: the no. 18, a cross-city service known as the 'Lawn Mower', was withdrawn in February 1940. The new form of transport had little chance, however, to show its paces: the last buses were leaving the Pillar for the suburbs as early as 9.30 in 1943.

It was a quiet land. The internal combustion engine had been virtually banished from the roads. The petrol ration for those engaged on essential services was miserly (for the ordinary citizen it was non-existent) and any abuse could lead to its immediate withdrawal. Mrs M. A. Fanning, the maternity nurse at Garristown, Co. Dublin, had her motor permit revoked on 3 September 1943 because the vehicle was allegedly used by a member of her family to transport workmen and farm machinery components. A taxi-driver would lose his permit if he carried his fares even to the proximity of a race-course if races were being run. Starters and racing officials were, however, allowed to proceed to race meetings in taxis, but not trainers, jockeys, or bookmakers, a nice distinction which drew the inevitable protest. Some people went to extreme lengths to acquire, if not the necessary permit, illegal petrol supplies in lieu. A Dublin gentleman who arranged to have coupons printed by a small Midland firm is said to have been apprehended on account of the omission of a síne fada from a capital A. Others explored the possibilities of The Renowned BELLAY GAS PRODUCER, the only producer (claimed the manufacturer, Auto Services Ltd., of Harcourt Street, Dublin)

1. That had a practical working experience behind it of OVER 15 YEARS ON THE CONTINENT
2. That has such a record of favourable running and performance that no alteration in design has been necessary for years
3. That has over 90 UNITS OPERATING SUCCESSFULLY THROUGHOUT EIRE
4. That filters the gas in such a way and to such an extent THAT NO IMPURITIES CAN ENTER THE ENGINE.

The Minister for Supplies, however, was not amused. 'Permits will not be granted for the fitting to private motor vehicles of gas producer plants ordered after 18.4.42', he said, 'unless the owner satisfies me that the vehicle is to be used for essential services.' It was small consolation to disgruntled car owners that he proceeded to fix a ceiling price of £8 for used adult bicycles, whilst agreeing to consider a request to make a similar Maximum Prices Order in respect of secondhand perambulators. It was shank's mare, unless ...

'Why not', some frivolous reader had suggested in *The Irish Times*, 'elephant and llama services ... why not let the dromedary earn his keep? It might even be possible to run a special gala zebra-line ...' First catch your zebra, but the ordinary stripeless quadruped was far from uncommon in Emergency Ireland, and horses of all shapes, sizes and conditions were rapidly pressed into service, harnessed to carts and conveyances of equally dubious and exotic provenance. 'Two bob a skull to Salthill. A shilling a leg', shouted the side-car drivers in Galway's Eyre Square. In County Limerick they went one better, with a stage coach service between the city and Adare complete with post-horn. As one passenger saw it: 'The good *Shamrock* coachman looked a picture in his bright scarlet coat—with the Adare crest on the shining brass buttons—fawn trousers, chamois gloves and biscuit-coloured raincoat. The light grey top-hat, with its immaculate blue ribbon, leant at a rakish angle over a deeply lined and wrinkled face in which shone the lightest of blue eyes ... This route's twenty miles were covered in three quarters of an hour, with three stops on the road ... The young and fair-haired Collector of Fares, Bugler and Guard looked as keen as mustard above his butterfly collar. Member of the Adare Brass Band, he taught himself the thirteen different Coaching Calls of his three-fcct-ten, silver-mounted coaching horn.' Myles na gCopaleen, predictably, was not impressed. 'I do not suppose that there is a decent man within the four walls of Ireland who has not been annoyed by the publicity given to this stage coach gag', he complained. 'Self-respecting Irishmen (wherever they may be, on land, or sea, or in the sky) will ask themselves what is the necessity for having, for instance, this horn-tooting business? It is colourful, you say ... Colourful? Every time I hear the word "colourful" I reach for my revolver.'

Colourful or not, the horse and equipage, together with the canal barge and the branch-line train, relived their hour of glory before passing finally into history. Fuel or no fuel, change was in the air. The tribunal which had been set up to rescue the railways from financial disaster finally reported and a Transport Bill passed on 29 November 1944 merged the Great Southern and the Dublin United Transport Co. into a new body with the initially puzzling title of Córas Iompair Eireann: 'They are now', said *Dublin Opinion*, 'referring to Transport employees as the Gentlemen of the Córas.' But for many of the new Board's services, decimated by fuel shortages and obsolescent equipment, the new overture proved to be a swan-song. The Ireland of Percy French vanished for good with the last of the Welsh steam coal, the Schull and Skibbereen and the snows of the post-Emergency winters.

"She must be vexed with me—she didn't ask for more than her ration."

# Here we are, there you are

*Tramp, tramp, tramp tramp! here they come along,*
*With rifles on their shoulders*
*And on the air a song,*
*A song which they are singing as they march right down*
    *the street,*
*A song which shows their courage and a soul that can't be*
    *beat.*
*chorus :*
*Here we are, there you are, why aren't you with us?*
*Aren't you ashamed of the clothes you're wearing?*
*There's room for me and room for you,*
*Together to see the whole thing through,*
*So come along and do your bit for Erin.*
*For here we are, there you are, why aren't you with us?*
*We've answered the call our country has been sending;*
*And if a foe would like to know*
*The length of our arm and the strength of our blow*
*The L.S.F., my boys, should be his warning.*

              A Marching Song for the L.S.F.

IN 1939 MESSRS W. D. AND H. O. WILLS, branch of the Imperial Tobacco Company of Great Britain and Ireland, issued a series of 40 cigarette cards entitled *Air Raid Precautions*. Number thirty-eight took as its subject The Civilian Anti-Gas School, which, provided by the Department of Defence, was at

Griffith Barracks, Dublin. 'The school trains anti-gas instructors for the public service, for local authorities and others', read the back of the card. 'Forty students are taken at a time and the course lasts two weeks. The picture shows business workers undergoing training. All are dressed in light protective oilskin clothing and are wearing either civilian duty or general civilian respirators. Those on the right are about to enter the gas chamber ...' The School, later to become the Air Raid Precautions School, was responsible for the training of over a thousand instructors in the first two years of the Emergency. The Air Raid Precautions Act, 1939, provided for the setting up of comprehensive schemes in Dublin, Cork, Limerick, Waterford, Wexford, Drogheda, Dundalk, Dun Laoghaire, Bray and Cobh, with skeleton schemes covering the rest of the country. The organisation attracted a hard core of enthusiastic volunteers, but the populace at large remained apathetic. Public bodies varied in their response: the Great Northern Railway fitted blue bulbs and switched them over when the trains crossed the Border; Messrs Thos Dockrell, Sons and Co. Ltd, of South Great Georges Street, Dublin, announced on 4 September 1939 that stocks of 'BLACK OUT BLACK' would be available the same afternoon, displaying a zeal that was at least equalled in Co. Mayo. 'In the town of Ballaghadereen', James Dillon told his fellow TDs on 19 September, 'some zealous soul went around about five weeks ago and put a tin canister over the bulb of every street lamp in town, with the result that the whole town was plunged into darkness except for a small restricted circle of light directly under the lamp. Now, the probability of sky glare from Ballaghadereen upsetting anybody is remote, and the probability of any person of ill-will desiring to bombard Ballaghadereen is remote'.

Mr Dillon was doing no more than reflecting the general feeling. The war was still a very long way away. 'Suppose a German U-Boat comes into our territorial waters,' asked James Hughes, TD, Carlow-Kildare, 'what are our coastal watchers going to do? Are they going to send for the *Muirchu* or have a pot at it with a rifle? What is the necessity for the whole scheme? ... Will they send word to Mr Chamberlain or vice-versa, will they send word to Herr Hitler if a British submarine comes in?'

But the fall of France in May 1940 altered the picture. The invasion of territorial waters, or of Irish territory itself, by one or other of the belligerents no longer seemed a matter for humorous speculation. In a broadcast to the nation on 1 June 1940, the Taoiseach announced the establishment of the Local Security Force, and appealed for recruits. Recruiting forms had already been dispatched to Gárda stations, and by 6 June 44,870 members had been enrolled. On the 22nd of the same month the new force was divided into two sections: 'A', to act as an auxiliary to the Army proper and 'B' to assist the Gardaí with auxiliary police duties. Training and control for both groups was placed in the hands of the Gárda Siochána. By August

11. Shaping a tradition: Naval Service MTB.

12. The loneliness of office: De Valera and Frank Gallagher,
director of the Government Information Bureau, in the
Taoiseach's room in Government Buildings.

13.  Spats and polish: preparing Air Corps Lysanders.

14. Emil Schmaltz, second from left, attended his brother's wedding in Germany shortly before his ship was torpedoed in the Bay of Biscay. He was rescued by the S.S. *Kerlogue* (see page 101) and interned in the Curragh.

15. Right there, Michael: 4–4–2T No. 274 of the former
Waterford, Limerick and Western Railway and escort.

16.  Níl aon tír gan teanga: the Gaelic League at the GPO.

17. Déanta in Éirinn: reconnaissance and armoured cars on AA defence.

18. Night mail: Pearse St., Dublin.

the total strength had reached 148,306, but had fallen again to 96,845 by 11 October and 84,252 as at 3 January 1941; the initial enthusiasm had been tempered somewhat by the equipment shortages and organisational muddles. 'The force was started last June', Roger Greene, a member of the 'B' Section in Cabinteely, Co. Dublin, wrote to General Mulcahy in January 1941, 'and we are still looking for facilities and equipment that should have been issued to us within a month of recruiting. We are apparently "nobody's child" and nobody gives a damn about us . . .' 'Manoeuvres held by the LSF in various parts of the country, even in contact with the military, have been regarded as very poor', the General himself had told the Defence Conference in the previous October, 'but what could be expected from a force organised around the police, and without any soldierly direction in County or other districts . . .'

Even allowing for the prejudice of the professional soldier, there was some measure of truth in the allegation. The force had got off to an uncertain start, and morale as well as efficiency was suffering. 'Now here is a matter which seems trivial at first sight but on consideration assumed more sinister proportions', wrote the editor of the *LSF Gazette* in October 1940. 'Lately certain members have been airing their grouses in the public Press. A number of these were quite legitimate but frankly, is this playing the game? Our "grumbles" do not concern non-members, so why spread them abroad? . . . There is no need to let the whole world know.'

The hurlers on the ditch, too, were not helping. The *Gazette* congratulated the men of Gorey who were rallying to the cause, but complained that 'there are yet in the town some die-hards—defeatists—who look askance at the efforts of the L.S.F. These men stand at the street corners and criticise—criticise men who have got what they lack. A virile nation has no use for such a type.'

Others, too, were failing to play their part in the eyes of the LSF. The *Gazette* reported that it had been swamped with letters 'from all parts of Eire complaining— and rightly too—about the action of many factories and offices. Some firms, among them a certain well-known factory in the South, actually displayed notices discouraging their men to join the Force and demanding that employees already members should resign . . .' It was not as if the war, particularly in the south, were still a remote abstraction. Three girls were killed by bombs, later confirmed as of German origin, at Campile creamery on 26 August 1940. On 25 October high explosive and incendiary bombs fell two miles from Rathdrum, Co. Wicklow. No one was injured. In the last incident of the year, at Shantonagh, near Carrickmacross, a farmer was slightly hurt. But the population as a whole still remained largely indifferent. A certain town council not 20 miles from Dublin graciously permitted the local LSF group to use the Town Hall for parades during the winter but passed the hat round on each occasion. Messrs Galligan's of Henry

Street, Dublin, were offering 'the new "Ardrí" Military Style coat, designed especially for LSF wear,' at 35/– (£1.75p) but the uniforms to wear under it were slow to appear. When at last the badges and armlets were supplemented with something conducive to a more military bearing, it did not meet with universal approval. The brown denims, reported Assistant Section Leader Thomas O'Keeffe, 'did much to damp the first fine frenzy. Strong men, who had announced their desire to tackle tanks single-handed, paled visibly when they saw how they were to be attired for the fray and many an aesthete, after a single glance, slipped out into the night and was never seen again.' In the Spring of 1942 the offending denims were replaced by green service uniforms.

The aim was to form one LSF Group—subdivided into Sections and Squads—in each area under the control of a Gárda station, and the range of duties was to include traffic control, communications, ARP, protective duties, first aid and transport. Night patrols in rural areas were to be organised from 10 p.m. to 6 a.m. and were to keep an eye out for parachutists or other untoward incidents. These basically civilian activities were maintained by 'B' group when, on 1 January 1941, 'A' Group was handed over from the Gárda to Army control, and was renamed the Local Defence Force, or LDF. 'B' Group retained the original title of Local Security Force or LSF.

The purpose was to create a more military type force for deployment in any invasion, the likelihood of which seemed to be increasing, but the improvement was not immediate. 'We have 100,000 LDF men with empty hands,' T. F. O'Higgins, TD, protested on 3 March 1941, 'as helpless as any civilians. We have 20,000 LDF men with rifles of a bore that limits the supply of ammunition to less than 100 rounds or about a couple of hours service.' And those that had weapons did not inspire absolute confidence. Dr T. O. Graham, who had a substantial property near Donnybrook, Dublin, permitted his lands to be used for LDF exercises. His wife was pleased to discover that the officer in charge was an old friend who had served with the Royal Dublin Fusiliers in the 1914–18 war. One Sunday afternoon she asked him to join them for a cup of tea. 'He told us he had been teaching them to shoot, and indeed we heard the guns and hoped we were all safely out of reach. I asked what he thought of his present Company. "Well", he said with a grin, "I hope if we do go into action I will be able to lead them from the rear".'

West British prejudice, perhaps. Neophytes there undoubtedly were, but there was no shortage of experience—hard-won experience at that. The 26th Rifle Battalion (City of Dublin Volunteers) was composed exclusively, both officers and men, of IRA veterans of the War of Independence 1916–21. And the skills of specialists were fully recognised. When 'A' Group came under Army control the various transport sections in the Dublin area were brought into Cathal Brugha barracks and became the 11th Transport Battalion, with a strength of approximately 700, under Captain George O'Doherty. The largest company, designated 'D', was made up of employees of the Dublin United Transport Co. The battalion had no independent transport; its task was to take over and operate vehicles commandeered in an emergency, and each driver was allocated one such vehicle, was aware of its location and where the keys were to be found. The 11th Cyclist regiment, which was formed on 25 May 1942, drew its strength of 600 from cycling clubs, An Oige, and the Department of Posts and Telegraphs. The 44th Squadron was Irish speaking.

Other specialised services had been brought into being or strengthened to meet actual or anticipated demands. In January 1940 the Irish Red Cross Emergency Hospitals' Supply Depot opened at 15, Lincoln Place, Dublin, and maintained a service for refugees from the North and Britain. Following the bombing of Belfast it was responsible for housing 785 victims for a period of six weeks. A year later the possibility of attacks on Dublin led the Government to introduce a limited evacuation scheme, covering members of families whose total income did not exceed £300 per annum and applying only to unaccompanied children of school age (6–14), children under school age (to be accompanied by their mother or other female relative) and expectant mothers. The scheme was to operate only in Dublin and the contiguous Dun Laoghaire County Borough, but it came in for criticism on the grounds that any attack, if it came, would not necessarily be directed at Dublin but could possibly involve the very areas to which the evacuees were to be directed.

As it happened, Dublin was to suffer the most from bombs accidentally or deliberately released over neutral Irish territory. In the early hours of the morning of 31 May 1941, Joseph Dempsey, a postman who lived at 578 North Circular Road, was awakened by a heavy thud. He switched on a flashlamp and saw a gaping hole in the ceiling over his head at the gable end of the house. He got up and ran into the street to discover that no. 582 had been completely demolished. Four bombs fell that night in the Dublin area, three in the vicinity of the North Strand and North Circular Road, and one, harmlessly, near the Dog Pond in the Phoenix Park. The three which fell in the city proper killed twenty-seven people, including seven members of the Browne family, wounded forty-five, completely destroyed twenty-five houses, amongst which was the premises of H. J.O'Neill, the undertakers who had charge of Paddy Dignam's funeral on Bloomsday, and rendered a further three hundred unfit for habitation. The noise of the explosions was heard as far away as Mullingar mental hospital. 'Even the outside world', proclaimed the *Irish Independent*, 'hardened as it has been by the daily toll of calamity on land and sea since the outbreak of this hideous war, has been shocked by the news that people could be killed by bombs in their houses in the capital of a neutral state.' The assumption was understandable in the circumstances. The Taoiseach moved a vote

# Nonsense—

we are not short of soap!

## We use—

# OKAY

and so save our soap

of sympathy with the bereaved in the Dáil and informed TDs that a protest had been made to the German government. There seemed little doubt as to the origins of the attack on this occasion, though when bombs had fallen on the South Circular Road in Dublin in the previous January an unofficial investigation in the area by the American Legation revealed that seven out of ten people believed them to be British.

On this occasion there were domestic as well as international repercussions. Early in June Patrick Cogan TD asked the Minister for Defence, 'if in view of the possibility of the recent air attacks on this country being due to our territory being mistaken for that of a belligerent State, steps will be taken either by special lighting or other distinctive signs, to indicate to belligerent aircraft the fact that this is neutral territory; if, further such measures will be adopted in all important centres throughout the country.'

The Minister suggested that the ordinary lighting of the country was considered sufficient to identify it, a response which did not satisfy James Dillon. 'Is it not true', he asked, 'that a one-eyed imbecile could see the difference between our cities and the belligerent's cities, if he wanted to see it, but we know that he damn well did not?'

Mr Dillon, as the one member of the Dáil outspokenly opposed to the policy of neutrality, lost no opportunity to attribute malice aforethought to the Germans in matters of this kind, though subsequent theories as to how these particular bombs came to be dropped have by no means been unanimous in their conclusions. At the time, the effect was simply to increase the sense of vulnerability. 'The intensity and effects of air raids which have been experienced during the present war were found to be in many ways unpredictable,' Seán Moylan, Parliamentary Secretary to the Minister for Defence, told the Dáil some three weeks after the North Strand incident. 'As a result of experience, it has been decided to increase considerably the strength of the fire-fighting service and the rescue service in Dublin. The fire-fighting service has been increased from 686 to 760. A national fire-fighting reserve consisting of six heavy-propelled units and six large trailer units is also being formed at a convenient distance from Dublin to provide a reserve for the whole country. The personnel for this service will be seventy-eight. The strength of the rescue service will be increased from 350 to 600.' Air raid shelters for 30,000 people were already in existence in Dublin city, and Mr Moylan announced that more were to be built in congested areas.

It did appear that the bombing attacks, from whatever source and for whatever reason, were increasing with something that looked like planned intensity. The year had opened with, on 2 January, incidents at Borris, Co. Carlow; Duleek, Co. Louth; Burrin village, Co. Wexford; Dublin; Drogheda; the Curragh; Julianstown, Co. Meath; and Kilmacanogue, Co. Wicklow—all involving no casualties except in the case of Borris where three people were killed and three injured. The following night,

3 January, bombs fell on the South Circular Road, Dublin, causing some injuries. A strengthening of the Civil Defence forces seemed only prudent in the circumstances.

Though incidents on the scale of the North Strand bombing were not, in fact, to occur again, the impact was slow to dissipate. A man was arrested and charged with stealing a pair of boots from one of the bombed houses and, as late as a year after the event, Mr John Maguire, of 1 Saint Joseph's Terrace, North Circular Road, was still attempting to secure compensation, under the Neutrality (War Damage to Property) Act 1941, for an overcoat which he lost whilst giving voluntary assistance on the night of the attack. The Minister for Finance informed Mr Alfie Byrne, who had raised the matter in the Dáil, that the missing garment was clearly outside the scope of the act and that he had been obliged to refuse to make any offer for compensation.

'I am sitting in the basement of "Dunedin", a house on Monkstown Avenue, nerve centre of Dun Laoghaire's vast Air Raid Precaution organisation', wrote an *Irish Independent* journalist. 'It is 10 o'clock on a mid-winter Saturday evening, zero hour for the largest night exercises ever held in the Borough. Eighty tons of reinforced concrete overhead and walled up around, make these headquarters safe even against a direct hit . . . Three minutes past ten . . . The first telephone bell rings, electrifying all to tense attention: the "attack" on Ireland's principal gateway has begun!'

Manoeuvres of one kind or another were, in the absence of the real thing, the basis of civil defence training, but it was at times difficult to establish clearly the boundaries between fantasy and reality. A lady in Mullingar was horrified one dark evening to see strange bedraggled figures emerging from the Royal Canal. She could not understand a word they were saying to one another—which was perhaps fortunate in the circumstances—and told a neighbour that she thought they were talking in morse code. During the 'Battle of Howth' on 27 July 1940 a stretcher squad from the 11th Field Ambulance left a 'patient' comfortable on his stretcher while they 'dodged into a hostelry for "just one"'. The account of the incident by Dr John Fleetwood and Vincent Walker continues: 'About an hour later they returned to an empty stretcher to which was pinned a note "Bled to death and gone home!"'

It was not the fault of the organisers if such occurrences detracted to some degree from the desired authenticity. The programme for this particular exercise, *Combined Manoeuvres by Group A and B, LSF Howth* was set out in meticulous detail:

'A state of emergency exists in Howth Area. Dispatch Riders (with cars or motor cycles) will be stationed at Gárda Barracks Howth. The Security Force has been mobilised. Group A members are stationed in Howth Castle Yard. Group B members are on patrol and communication duty.

'The Security Force Defending Army will wear white band on right arm. "Paratroops" will wear a red band on right arm. Umpires will wear a white armlet with a red band and other neutrals a blue armlet . . . The Howth and Sutton Nursing Division, St John's Ambulance, under Miss Gaisford St Lawrence, and the Bayswater Emergency Hospital Staff under Dr W. Chapman, Medical Officer and Mrs Richardson, Matron, will act as the First Aid Detachment.

'Fifth Columnists who may be male or female will be appointed and will receive secret instructions, and be given special identification papers. Both forces are warned to ensure that no persons should be permitted to co-operate with the manoeuvres unless they carry L.S.F. membership cards, or special identification papers signed by the Adjutant. Fifth Columnists may, if instructed, wear white armlet, but may not wear umpires' or neutral armlet.

'Umpires will receive detailed instructions. They will be issued with typed labels which they will issue to troops on both sides. Members receiving labels will tie them on their coat buttons and act as follows:

RED LABEL: Killed in Action. Report to Q.M. Howth Castle for further instructions.
GREEN LABEL: Seriously wounded. Stretcher case. To be treated and evacuated by Red Cross Organisation. (Nature of wound will be stated).
BUFF LABEL: Light wound, after First Aid will resume duty with their force.
BLUE LABEL: Prisoners.'

'The main attack', as Fleetwood and Walker describe it, 'developed on the Defenders' left wing, the belt of trees . . . being used as cover, and so well did the Invaders use this cover that they were actually able to advance to a position from which to direct enfilade fire on the whole frontal advanced line of the Defenders and these men were marked out as Casualties. In this case the Advanced Defence Line left its flank completely exposed. This left the position of defence in the main line, and the right flank defence outpost retired prematurely to help ward off the attack which now seemed to be developing from the left front. It was then that the lady "Fifth Columnist" was enabled to penetrate the main line of defence but was captured by an alert sentry in the "nick of time" . . .'

'Props' included dummy bombs (linen bags filled with sawdust), 'rattles if obtainable to indicate machine gun fire', dummy explosives, hammers, shovels and pioneer tools.

'The Howth Manoeuvre was one of the most talked-of happenings in 1940', say Fleetwood and Walker. 'Criticism was levelled at it by the experts, with a view to the improvement of military technique. The corner-boys, educated and otherwise, fouled their own nests, by passing the usual inane remarks . . .' But they added: 'As a piece of recruitment propaganda the Howth Manoeuvre succeeded beyond anyone's wildest dreams.' 'When I first heard what it was proposed to attempt', de Valera wrote to Professor Bayley Butler, the G.S.O.1., 'I thought it was altogether too ambitious for a newly-established Force which had not what I considered the necessary time for training. The event showed that I was mistaken, and that with the excellence of your staff work you had been able to overcome the difficulties which I had feared. I am glad to know that you and all who participated in the exercises were pleased with the result of your work, and I would like you to convey to the members of your staff my admiration and appreciation.' 'It was a good day', concluded Anthony McGinty, who was Adjutant General of the Defenders: 'and the men got the mucking about they would get and expect in a real action.'

Apart from large scale exercises such as this, test mobilisations were held regularly—often at uncomfortable hours of the night. In standing armies where troops are billeted in centralised areas the problem of mobilisation is simple but, as Fleetwood and Walker observe: 'In a force like the LDF such a system is manifestly impossible. Members of such a small unit as a ten man section may live miles apart and their common equipment, stretchers, machine guns, even rifles in some cases, must be stored in a central depot ... After much trial and error the LDF generally adopted the "snowball" system of calling out. In this scheme the original call goes from the responsible military authority to the most easily available LDF man ... the latter now calls two or more other men, who in turn call two or more and so on rather on the "big fleas have little fleas" system ...'

Such mobilisations were also the prelude to full-scale night exercises. 'Thousands of LDF men from the Dublin commands took up position last night all around the city', reported the *Irish Independent* on 29 June 1941, 'as the first line of Dublin's defence in a large-scale "attack" which opened in the early hours of the morning.'

But, as the external dangers receded, so, inevitably, did the enthusiasm, if not in the ranks, in higher places. Following a Defence Conference discussion late in 1944 as to the future of the LSF, General Mulcahy noted that 'The Ministerial attitude seemed to be that they could in fact be disbanded, but they wanted to present medals to them and they did not like to disband them in 1944 and to look for them again in 1946 or 1947 to give them medals.'

On 29 November 1944 the Minister for Defence announced in the Dáil that the Government had decided that two medals would be struck—one to be awarded to those who served during the Emergency in the Defence Forces, Chaplaincy Service and Army Nursing Service and the other to those who served in the voluntary services.

*It's been a tough show but it will be something to talk about later, when in years to come the 42nd boast of how they waded across the flooded Dodder and the 41st talk of their prowess on the battle course at Gormanstown.*

" Glory be ! The Glimmer Man ! "

# *Only like hens scratching*

*Let us be honest about this unity of the people. There is no such thing as unity of the people. There is a pretence of unity.*

PATRICK MCGILLIGAN, TD

*Without any negotiations or clear cut arrangements we have agreed to a political truce.*

T. F. O'HIGGINS, TD

'*Why do you call your dog "Franchise"?*'
'*Because we get so few chances to exercise him.*'

Dublin Opinion

WHEN THE Emergency period began, Fianna Fáil, under de Valera, had held political power for some seven years. The election of 1938 had given them a total of seventy-seven seats and a comfortable working majority. In the circumstances the Taoiseach saw no reason to yield to the intermittent demands from the Opposition parties, Fine Gael and Labour, for a national or coalition government. Even had he agreed, however, such an administration would have been a doubtful starter. The legacy of the Civil War was still very much in evidence, so much so that there was very little contact, social or political, between the representatives of the opposing sides in the Dáil. An electoral challenge was equally out of the question. For good or ill, de Valera had enunciated a firm policy of neutrality that had rallied virtually the whole country behind him. In the Dáil, the lone figure of James Dillon, who was to be expelled from Fine Gael for his views, was the only representative voice raised against it. The Opposition knew that to force an election, on whatever issue, would be to court annihilation.

This was not a position that they could be expected to hold with any degree of enthusiasm, but, with the suspension of the normal pattern of party politics (except, of course, in the Dáil; but not everything that was said there passed the censorship) they had little choice. In practice they were virtually powerless to intervene in the course of events, and the establishment of the Defence Conference on 24 May 1940 only served to rub salt in the wound. 'An examination of the Minutes of the Defence Conference since August or September last will show that we have been only like hens scratching' General Mulcahy complained in February 1941, and, a year later his Fine Gael colleague Patrick McGilligan re-echoed the sense of frustration. 'As far as this Dáil had decided' he said, 'two representatives of this party and two representatives of the Labour party, joined by members of the Government party, meet in conference to discuss certain matters of defence. Outside there is no such thing as unity. This conference has been used through the country as a means of pretending to the people that there is something like a national government in the country. We know that this is not so.'

It is doubtful whether de Valera ever intended it to be anything more than a talking shop and a gesture towards an appearance of national political unity. As Dr T. F. O'Higgins complained to his chief, W. T. Cosgrave, in November 1940, the truce between Fianna Fáil and Fine Gael was agreed to 'on the understanding that through the medium of the Defence Conference or by direct contact there would be consultation before any grave pronouncement would be made affecting foreign relations or defence'. In practice this never happened. It is difficult, indeed, to see how it could ever have been put into effect, given the views held by the Fine Gael representatives, which were for the most part seriously at variance with the Government's policy. On 13 November 1940 Senator Mulcahy made notes of the points he wished to emphasise at the forthcoming meeting of the Conference. One was a total resistance to any attack from Germany in expectation of British assistance. 'But in the case of British aggression', he noted, 'we would find it conscientiously impossible to recommend the continuance of military resistance.' De Valera's policy, in theory at least, was to oppose any invader with equal persistence. 'The Government mentality with regard to Britain and Northern Ireland is fantastic', the General had complained some months previously. Earlier again, in June 1940, the Fine Gael representatives had originated a proposal for a unified command for the defence of the whole island—a French/British/Irish force supplied with material by the United States and operating under a French General with French officers. It is perhaps not surprising, after the unveiling of this picturesque programme, that the Conference found itself limited to matters of purely local significance with no bearing whatsoever on overall strategy or even interim tactics.

The original members of the Conference were, from the Government: the Minister for the Co-Ordination of Defensive Measures, Frank Aiken, who acted as chairman; the Minister for Justice, Gerald Boland; the Minister for Defence, Oscar Traynor. From Fine Gael: Senator Mulcahy, Deputy T. F. O'Higgins. From Labour: Deputies Norton and Davin. There would appear to have been little variation in its composition, at least until late 1943, but meetings became very irregular; there was no meeting in 1944 until 15 December. On 25 April 1945 the Taioseach informed Deputy Oliver Flanagan, in response to a question in the Dáil, that the Conference was in abeyance and would shortly be dissolved, but doggedly refused on a linguistic technicality to name the members. It had clearly outlived whatever usefulness it had possessed.

'The Dáil makes me think of the Supervisors' meetings that I used to report in Monroe County when I worked in the Rochester Union and Advertiser', H. E. David Gray, US Minister to Eire, reported to President Franklin Roosevelt. If this were true, it was not entirely the fault of that body. For perfectly plausible security reasons directly related to any compromise, or the appearance of any compromise of the nation's neutrality, most attempts by Deputies to raise matters of national or international significance were frustrated by government ministers and the vacuum was inevitably filled by arguments over domestic issues of the most limited local interest. There were many allegations by the Opposition of the Government's abusing its powers not only in the matter of refusing debate, but of manipulating the censorship for party political ends. True or false, there was little Fine Gael and Labour could do about it, other than protest, until the life of the 10th Dáil had run its course.

The election would normally have been due in 1943. In that year de Valera, pleading special circumstances, introduced a bill to prolong the life of the parliament by one year, but, in the face of strong opposition, withdrew it on 5 May. The election duly took place on 22 June, eight gallons of petrol being allocated to each candidate nominated for a constituency, and Fianna Fáil was returned with 67 seats—still the largest party but without a clear majority. There was a new party in the house: Clann na Talmhan, the farmers' party, with ten seats ('I lost me money on Whirlaway in the Derby, but got it all back on Clann na Talmhan in the Election', crowed a cartoon character of the time). The Clann had been in existence for some time ('Sons of the Soil, yer name is mud!' jeered *Dublin Opinion* in 1940) but it had now emerged as a serious political force. Less serious, perhaps, was the new Monetary Reform party,

# IRELAND IS CALLING You! Join the army NOW!

now represented in Dáil Eireann by its founder and president Oliver Flanagan, or Oliver Gold-myth as he was quickly dubbed. He equally quickly made his mark, being reproved by the Ceann Comhairle for attempting to introduce the subject of monetary reform into the debate on the appointment of the Taoiseach. Four women had stood for election as independents, including Miss Hanna Sheehy-Skeffington in South Dublin, and all were beaten. Three others were successful: Mrs Rice, Mrs Redmond and Mrs Reynolds, known as the Three Rs or the Silent Sisters, and all widows of former TDs.

Mr de Valera was again leader of the Government, but, even though the Fine Gael representation had also been reduced—from 45 to 32—he felt himself to be in a position of weakness. And the temper of the new Dáil was somewhat different from that of the old. Docility had given way to a refusal to be easily put off. For the Taoiseach, accustomed to having his own way, this was an unwelcome development. 'Might I say, in connection with questions I have been asked,' he charged on 1 March 1944, 'that certain Deputies are obviously specialising at the moment in asking questions which appear to be aimed at embroiling us with one set or other of the belligerents. They are, in some cases, so designed that it is extremely difficult to give an answer that will not appear to indicate a siding by us with one set or other of the belligerents. They are often very tendentious in the framing and the mere putting of them on the Order Paper is tendentious.' He went as far as to threaten to seek power from the Ceann Comhairle or other authority to exclude such questions, whilst at the same time affirming his belief in the right of every Deputy to freedom of speech.

It was becoming clear that the situation was unstable—or at least not stable enough for the taste of the Taoiseach. Following an acrimonious debate on the Transport Bill, in which charges were levied of corruption in Stock Exchange dealings, the Government was defeated. On 10 May 1944 Seán Lemass moved the adjournment of the Dáil *sine die*.

The prospect of another election aroused very little enthusiasm among the Opposition parties. 'I desire to place on record the considered and emphatic protest of this Party at the action of the Taoiseach and the Government in plunging this country into an unnecessary general election at the most dangerous and critical weeks the people of this country were ever asked to live through', said Dr T. F. O'Higgins. This was no mere hyperbole; the affair of the American note had shaken the country (see page 138) and Britain had recently introduced a virtual blockade in preparation for the opening of the Second Front. 'After astute manoeuvring, politically corrupt practices and unnational activity', continued O'Higgins, 'guided by political exegencies, rather than consideration for the safety and security of the country, opportunists decided to take advantage of the failing health of a great figure in order to cheat Parliament of the right of fulfilling its destiny.'

The allusion was to the ailing President, Douglas Hyde, then 84 years of age. Mr Norton, for the Labour Party, spoke on the same theme. 'High treason was committed in the Park last night', he said. 'We found the Taoiseach arriving in the darkness of the night, in the house of an aged man whom everyone knows to be in anything but a perfect state of health. One can imagine the scene—the Taoiseach full of venom against a democratic Parliament which had unseated his Government. One is left to imagine the tone in which the demand for a dissolution was presented to the aged man in the Park last night.'

One was not left for long. James Dillon had always reacted strongly against the dominant personality of the Taoiseach. 'I objected to his sending for me, I did not want to be influenced by him', Richard Mulcahy had said in 1941, when de Valera had summoned him over an earlier crisis involving the American Minister. In the case of Dillon any such influence was of a patently negative character. 'The Fianna Fáil doctrine is that the Taoiseach hates politics' he now told the Eleventh Dáil in its dying moments: 'that he does not understand them, that he recoils from engaging in them and longs to govern this country from the Olympian calm of the Institute of Higher Studies, his dearest pride and joy, with an Olympian patience that understands everything and, understanding everything, forgives everything. Well, it is a quare picture of the gentleman in a motor car, blazing through the night up to the Viceregal Lodge to get poor President Hyde out of his bed to sign the dissolution: the Olympian calm, the Olympian patience, the Institute of Higher Studies and the President in his nightshirt, tottering down the stairs to sign the dissolution.'

The reluctance of the opposition parties to welcome the election was amply justified by the result. Fianna Fáil was returned with 76 seats and a safe overall majority of 14.

'If the Dáil is asked to discuss anything on the grounds that the Oireachtas may not be able to meet', Richard Mulcahy wrote on 3 August 1940, 'the Dáil must be informed from what direction dangers threaten: (a) Germany, (b) Britain, (c) Northern Ireland, (d) Internal (IRA). These were the original four. Have any been added. Has there been an addition (e) Internal (Social)?'

The General was not indulging in idle speculation. On 31 May an undercover agent posing as a member of the St Vincent De Paul Society and professing anti-Jewish leanings had infiltrated a meeting held at the Red Bank Restaurant, d'Olier Street, Dublin. The tone of the assembly was markedly pro-Nazi and anti-Jewish. His cover was accepted and he was invited to be present at a further meeting, which was held at 7, Slane Road, Kimmage, according to his unsigned and otherwise unidentified report, the home of a Mr Griffin. At this meeting it was decided that in future the Organisation would be known as the 'Anti-Christian Association': this was necessary, it was explained, to 'cloak matters up'. 'We were given tea, sandwitches, buscuits (sic) and cigarettes', the report continues. Griffin announced that a number of their supporters had been arrested and gave the names of Alex McCabe; Liam Walsh; Holden; O'Connor and Hand, a German. With reference to Holden it was stated that he was a member of Fianna Fáil and 'that a political string could be pulled'.

The bogus Vincent de Paul man attended a further meeting at the Swiss Chalet Restaurant, Merrion Row, Dublin on 26 June. From here he reported that 'The founders of the party were General O'Duffy; Liam Wlash; Seamus Bourke and a Mr O'Callaghan, a Civil Servant who publishes the German War News. He was arrested and released.' The name was, he learnt to be not the Anti-Christian Association but the People's National Party, run on National Socialist lines. It was stated at the meeting that a German invasion was expected on 15 July, and that they were 'ready to facilitate the German Army in every respect'.

If the embryo Irish Nazi party had little chance to assist the Germans, other political groups out of sympathy with the declared policy of neutrality fared little better. The intelligence service, a combination of the Gárda Special Branch and the Army Intelligence section, was small but effective, and apart from their activities directed against agents introduced into the country from outside, which is considered elsewhere, their main concern was with the IRA. 'This moment, when small nations throughout Europe are devoting all their effort to strengthening national unity', de Valera told the nation early in 1940, 'is a moment that a group in this country has chosen to attempt to destroy our organised life.' His answer in the face of this threat was to arrest IRA members and known sympathisers and intern them. One of the first to suffer this treatment was Mairtín O Cadhain, who was picked up in Parnell Square, Dublin in October 1939 and confined to Cell 31 in Arbour Hill detention barracks. He found himself in what might in other circumstances have been quite a stimulating atmosphere—'Níl aon teanga dhá raibh i Babel nach bhfuil anseo dhá muineadh againn', he wrote, 'Gaelige, Fraincis, Spainnis, Gearmainis, Laiden, Breatnais, Briotainis . . .', but he was not left long to appreciate it. The acute legal mind of Seán McBride had discovered a loophole in the act and O Cadhain, along with other political prisoners was released at Christmas. He was not long at liberty, however, for a new measure was introduced early in 1940 and in April he was arrested at the graveside of Tony d'Arcy, who had died on hunger strike, and interned in the Curragh—'Sibéir na hEireann', as he described it, until July 1944.

Other political prisoners were sent to Portlaoise and Mountjoy, where, according to Oliver Flanagan TD, seven women were imprisoned 'without any charge or crime in the wide world'. He listed them as Maire O'Sullivan, Eileen

O'Kelly, Mollie and Pat Gallagher, Maggie O'Halloran, Maggie Doyle and Patricia Kelly. In Portlaoise, Seán McCaughey, who was arrested in September 1941, refused to wear prison clothes and was kept naked in solitary confinement. Hunger strikes and executions—a hangman had to be imported from Britain—gave the Government some of its most difficult moments. Protestors against the execution of George Plant on 3 March 1942 showered Dublin with pamphlets from the top of Nelson's Pillar on the following St Patrick's Day. The previous year the inhabitants of Dublin's sedate suburb of Rathmines had been startled by the appearance in their midst of a man in chains hobbling down Castlewood Avenue to give himself up to the local Guards. He was Stephen Hayes, an IRA chief who had been suspected of informing on the organisation and had been held under duress whilst a 'confession' was extracted from him. This incident, and the violence which followed, did not improve the IRA's public image.

Other dissident groups were more easily dealt with. There was concern over the banning of the *Wolfe Tone Annual* in October 1943 (whether for being too close to or too far away from the ideals of 1798 is difficult to discern) and on the eve of the 1944 Hurling Final Gardaí were constrained to remove a banner with an inscription demanding a 32 COUNTY PARTITION AND REPUBLICAN PLEBECITE which had been erected across Russell Street adjacent to the Canal Bridge entrance to Croke Park (Cork, 2–13, beat Dublin, 1–2). The Army, on the other hand, apparently looked with a tolerant eye upon the owner of Killiney Castle, Co. Dublin who in the early days of the Emergency would appear from the basement, the rest of the building having been commandeered, to hoist the tricolour on the occasion of the then-frequent German victories.

For Seán Citizen, however, there were realities closer to home. Lacking the stimulus of active participation in the war, the economy was at best ticking over, and for many people the Emergency was a time of genuine hardship which the politicians could do little to alleviate. As early as December 1939 there was a national protest by the farming community following widespread discontent over farm prices, and in May 1941 Seán Lemass ('Mr Lemass might be called our "blood and tears" minister, where Mr de Valera is our "God-is-good" minister', suggested *The Bell*) shocked the country with his Wages Standstill Order, which effectively froze incomes for the duration. 'Lemass's standstill order was as harsh an ordinance as any of my generation had endured in a lifetime', said Roibéard O Faracháin, who was Talks Officer in Radio Eireann at the time. 'As bitter a blow as could have been struck at a young man beginning the rearing of a family, the buying of a house and all the rest . . . The reason why they got away with it was that the Irish people were so grateful to

19. Early days: regulars and reservists step together.

20.  Gas production: Great Southern Railways keep going.

21. Consultation in Co. Cork, 1940. The signposts, together with the German-style helmet, were shortly to figure on the Emergency casualty list.

22. Hard-won warmth: saving turf in the Dublin mountains.

23.  Transported: last lorry for Tipperary.

24. Me and mine: family group with exotic hardware,
Brittas Bay, Co. Wicklow.

25. Dublin defences: 3·7 in. AA guns, 1941.

26. Gloster Gladiator and Air Corps gunners.

God that bombs were not raining down on them, as they were on so many peoples, that they accepted this continuous attrition of their standstill earnings, with all the grinding concomitant deprivations, humbly and gratefully . . .'

Not all of them—the trade unions for one, were bitterly opposed to the measure. And there were those who were in no position either to accept or reject the measure, those who had no job and little prospect of one. For many the only solution was the emigrant boat. Britain was eager for workers to man her industries. 'The Irish government of the day had made an agreement with the British Ministry of Labour which shipped us into exile,' Donal Foley, who was one of those who went, recalled. 'The train to Dublin was packed with people from Waterford, county and city. At Kilkenny the platform was crowded with young people, the mothers clinging onto them loath to let them go and anxious to get the last seconds of their companionship. So it was at all the little stations, until finally Kingsbridge. This was neutral Ireland . . .'

The Government quickly realised, however, that this exodus of the unemployed, however useful it might be for relieving them of serious embarrassment, had its unfavourable aspect. Not all of those heading east were jobless; many agricultural workers were finding that they could make more money more easily in the factories of Birmingham. An order was thus introduced prohibiting persons ordinarily resident outside towns of 5000 population and over from going to Britain to work; this applied particularly to men in certain areas who had, in the words of Seán O'Grady, the Parliamentary Secretary to the Minister for Industry and Commerce, 'a minimum experience of agricultural or turf-cutting operations'. There were, naturally, anomalies. Mr O'Grady promised to enquire into the case of Michael Clarke, of Drumboat, Iniskeen, Dundalk, who, according to the information available to him, was 'a farmer with considerable agricultural experience who lives and works on his own holding. He may not, therefore, be facilitated to emigrate as he resides in one of the areas from which the emigration of men with agricultural experience is prohibited.' Michael Clarke was, in fact, according to James Dillon, a man who had spent his entire life as a dock labourer in Liverpool and was anxious to resume his regular and familiar employment.

One major and serious attempt was made to tackle the unemployment problem at home. Following experiments made by the Turf Development Board in the establishing of a Labour Camp (the term had not then fallen into international disrepute) at Clonsast, the Office of Public Works submitted a proposal to the Army for the creation of a Labour Battalion which would draw its strength from unemployed men between the ages of 18 and 25. 'These may be regarded as the hard core of the social problem of the adolescent unemployment', a Department of Finance memorandum had stated. 'They represent a real danger of economic and social degeneration to both themselves and the community. The remedy for this evil is simply employment under suitable and disciplined conditions.'

This Orwellian panacea took the form of the Construction Corps, An Cór Déantais, which was established in October 1940 with the twin (and, it emerged, incompatible) aims of social rehabilitation and the furtherance of work of national importance. As a senior Army officer put it: 'If you are going to inculcate the three Rs into illiterates (the illiteracy rate was extremely high) in twelve months you can make up your mind that it cannot be done to a bog-draining accompaniment. Nor if you give a man hard physical exercises during the day can you expect him to register enthusiasm over evening lessons.'

At its peak in 1943 the Corps attained a strength of approximately 2,000, the target of five battalions never being reached. It was hampered by muddled thinking as to its aim and purpose (six months after its establishment there was virtually no work for it to do), inexperience and ignorance of the social problems involved and, stemming from these two deficiencies, the disapproval, amounting to detestation, of both the regular Army and the civilian population with which it came into contact. Most of the boys were recruited from deprived urban backgrounds and found life in remote barracks in equally deprived rural areas almost impossible to come to terms with. Some work of solid and lasting value was achieved (the Corps built the runways at Gormanstown and Baldonnel (Casement) air bases) but the scheme was hastily and inadequately prepared and, with some notable exceptions, generally mismanaged by people who were by both training and temperament ill-equipped to build an organisation on the model of the German Labour Force which had provided part, at least, of the initial impetus.

The few crumbs of comfort falling into the laps of the working population had little effect on the general standard of living. 'Children will now be referred to as the half-crowning happiness of married life', a wit suggested on the introduction of the 2s 6d ($12\frac{1}{2}$p) per week Children's Allowance. It was a drop in the bucket; letters from Britain containing emigrants' remittances had become an essential part of the home economy and were awaited each week with eagerness and anxiety. There were scenes in the Dáil when Alfie Byrne, amongst others, protested against near-starvation conditions in the city's slums. But however bad things might be at home, most people admitted, as the war overseas reached its climax, that they were far worse elsewhere. On 1 December 1944 de Valera moved in the Dáil the allocation of £100,000 to the International Red Cross for the alleviation of distress in Italy. He was supported by General Mulcahy for Fine Gael, Mr Blowick for Clann na Talmhan, and Mr Norton, speaking for Labour, who said: 'Our own people have their problems at home. No matter what these problems are or how acute they might be in an economic sense, I think no one will grudge extending a helping hand to those who are the victims of the conditions which have been so luridly described to us by the Taoiseach this evening.' The sole dissenting voice was that of Mr Oliver Flanagan, who suggested that the money could have been put to better use at home. 'I would ask Deputy Flanagan to remember that there is no comparison whatever between the distress in Italy and the distress in this country', Mr Anthony retorted. 'Even the poorest of the poor here are far better off than those who are suffering in other countries as a result of the great war.'

On 8 March 1945 the Taoiseach told the Dáil that the French authorities had warmly accepted the offer of an Irish Red Cross Hospital. Amongst those who subsequently served with the unit at Rouen was an Irishman who had spent the war first in Paris, which he left just ahead of the Gestapo, and Vichy France: Samuel Beckett.

" My husband wants it for the sitting-room. He's been shot three times by emergency coal !"

FUEL SHORTAGE

# *The lonely sea and the sky*

*The third of September 1939 will always stand out in maritime history not as the day on which the Second World War was declared ... but as the day realisation dawned in Ireland that the country was surrounded by water and that the sea was of vital importance to her. Neutrality was declared with just nothing whatever to defend it with in the internationally vital area of the territorial sea ...*

CAPTAIN T. MACKENNA, NS

*You don't know what suffering is until you've been the one Protestant among 32 Roman Catholics in the Dublin Bay Port Control.*

CPO THE HON. PATRICK CAMPBELL

VARIOUS arguments have been advanced to explain Ireland's pointed indifference to the seas around her shores in the modern historical period. Up to the time of the British departure it is fairly easy to lay the blame on the country's having little say in its own economic destiny, but that certainly does nothing to explain the continuing indifference that was manifest up to the eve of the second world war. The Australian parallel is interesting; that country, too, was notably reluctant to develop its own maritime tradition, all things pertaining to ships and the sea having been since the establishment of the first colony firmly in the hands of Great Britain. If British primacy disinclined certain Australians of anti-Imperial

94

tendencies or background to pursue the sea as a calling, as John Bach suggests in his *Maritime History of Australia*, the case of Ireland might argue a similar response. For whatever reason, the new State seemed content enough to leave its maritime concerns in the hands of the former colonial power, both as regards merchant shipping and naval defence. The events of 1939 were to provide a rude awakening and inspire precipitate action.

Vivian Mercier, writing in *The Bell* in 1944, on '*Dublin Opinion*'s six jokes,' categorised number three as 'The Irish navy joke, descending from all those fine old jests about the Swiss navy', and suggested that even the new flotilla of motor torpedo boats would fail to spoil the *Muirchu* joke. The *Muirchu*, a gunboat built in the Liffey Dockyard in 1908, began life as the *Helga II* under the British administration, shelling the Post Office in Easter week with devastating inaccuracy, and was handed over on 7 August 1923 to the Free State government who renamed her and placed her under the control of the Department of Agriculture and Fisheries. Her duties as a fishery protection vessel must have been somewhat impaired by her alleged inability to function in anything but calm water. As one variant of *Dublin Opinion* joke no. 3 put it:

> Oh don't go out tonight, Daddy!
> The Captain's Boy he cried,
> Oh don't go out tonight, Daddy,
> There's a ripple on the tide!

This doubtful asset constituted, together with the equally suspect *Fort Rannoch*, the entire strength of the naval forces at 3 September 1939. In the words of Captain MacKenna, 'We were on our own with nothing but a 1908 vintage Fishery Protector armed with a three-pounder and solid shot, to look after 5,127 square miles of the then territorial sea on a perimeter of 783 miles and a coastline of 1970 miles.'

Quite apart from the dearth of ships, a naval service as such did not exist. On 29 August a 'Coastwatching Service' was established with headquarters in Portobello Barracks in Dublin and by 1 September thirty-four men had been recruited and eight Look Out Posts established between Cahore Point, Co. Wexford and Dursey Head, Co. Kerry. On 3 September the service was renamed 'The Marine and Coastwatching Service', and the Government gave orders for a complete chain of Look Out Posts to be established and manned. Dublin port was also declared closed, a seaplane tender and other small vessels being requisitioned from the Air Corps to enforce this edict. Two Motor Torpedo Boats had in fact been ordered from Thorneycroft in England and an order was hastily placed for four more. Before the end of the year the *Muirchu* and the *Fort Rannoch* had been formally taken over from

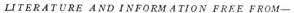

the Department of Agriculture and Fisheries. The first motor torpedo boat was delivered on 8 January of the following year and commissioned by Lieutenant J. Carey on 29 January. The embryonic service had received its first Commanding Officer, Colonel A. T. Lawlor, on 3 January; he, like the commander of the MTB, bore an army rank. It was not until 7 June of the same year that the Defence Forces (Temporary Provisions) Act 1940 established marine ranks and ratings.

The order for MTBs was not completed until 24 December 1942, when the last one of the six was commissioned. This brought the strength of the Marine Service (it had been separated from the Coastwatching Service on 17 July 1942) to two patrol vessels (the *Muirchu* and *Fort Rannoch*), a 'mine planter' (SS *Shark*), a training ship and the six MTBs: and at this it remained for the duration. It was a paltry enough force, but at least one journalist, spending a week with the Marine Service, succeeded in conveying the impression of almost limitless naval potential. 'The following day was given over to manoeuvres', wrote J. B. O'Sullivan: 'We watched these from the fo'c's'le head of a patrol vessel. Midget objects in the distance drew steadily closer and revealed themselves as a flotilla of Motor Torpedo Boats, spread out in double-echelon formation. The menacing throb of their engines came louder and louder to us across the water, then began to fade as the vessels passed us, tearing the waves apart and spreading them out in valleys of surf behind them.

'Then came a "line abreast" formation, Aldis lamps signalling distance and speed from the flotilla leader to each vessel.

'Then in "line ahead" a flotilla passed the prow of our boat and each swung round in an arc to come up in "line abreast" . . .'

. . . or the magnification of the six MTBs.

Minefields were laid in 1941 in the Cork harbour area and the approaches to Waterford, and one of the tasks which the Marine Service shared with the Army Ordance Corps was the disposal of drifting mines. The Army dealt with those washed ashore, whilst the Navy exploded those sighted at sea with rifle fire. Hawlbowline, in Cork Harbour, had been occupied as the Service's principal base in July 1940, and a recognition of the strategic importance of the Cork harbour area was further indicated by the presence of the bucket-dredger *Owenacurra*, filled with explosives and anchored at Passage West for use as a block-ship if required. At critical moments during the Emergency years she was kept under steam and ready to sail.

'It is our job, as the Port Control Service', wrote CPO The Hon. Patrick Campbell, 'to board incoming vessels and give them a clearance signal into the port. This looks like a fascinating profession, from O'Connell Bridge, but it cools down as you get into it. We used to get some good ships at first, white Norwegian tankers, greasy Egyptian tramps, Greeks from Rosario and the River Plate, but now (1943) we enjoy a few regular colliers and our own Irishmen in from overseas.' Though Port Control existed in a rudimentary form from the outset, it was not until the Emergency Order of 1 July 1940 setting up Competent Port Authorities and Port Control and Examination Service that it was really effective. The Competent Port Authorities, who were usually the local harbourmasters and who were given temporary commissions in the Marine Service, functioned in Lough Swilly, Sligo, Galway, Limerick, Fenit, Bantry, Cork, Waterford, Rosslare, Dun Laoghaire, Dublin, Drogheda and Dundalk. Lough Swilly had the task of dealing with the battered merchantmen limping in from the North West approaches; they had a base at Fort Dunree, a strength of ten, and a single motor launch, the *Eileen*. Cork's headquarters were in Fort Camden, and the muster of eighteen had the use of a succession of craft, the third being involved in the worst Marine Service disaster of the Emergency. On the night of 12 December 1942, this vessel, known for some reason as the 'feather plucker', was, together with the Cork Harbour pilot, caught in the propellors of the SS *Irish Poplar* (ex *Vassilos Destounis*) and a Petty Officer, two leading seamen and an AB together with one man from the pilot were lost. There was a Force 8 gale blowing at the time, but the sole survivor managed to swim to Spike Island where he raised the alarm.

The headquarters of Dublin and Dun Laoghaire Port Control was Atlantic Hall in the Alexandra Basin. There was a total strength of forty-eight, and the examination vessel was the former Dublin Port and Docks tug MV *Noray*, thirty-six feet long, powered by an elderly diesel and carrying a complement of six. She was stationed permanently at Dublin Bar. Her crew were at sea for twenty-four hours at a stretch. 'Our job', recalled Patrick Campbell, 'was to search every incoming vessel, to check against the arrival of what Standing Orders called "Unauthorised Persons". The boarding party was armed with 1914 Lee-Enfield rifles and in the beginning we used a rowing boat to cover the distance between the *Noray* and the ship. It was dangerous and useless work.'

Campbell and his colleagues were at times instructed to turn a blind eye on certain B&I boats from Liverpool, which were carrying weapons for the army. In their shore patrols and quayside ship examinations (all weapons had to be removed and the radio sealed before the visiting ship was allowed to begin loading or unloading) the Port Control was assisted by men of the Maritime Inscription, a volunteer force which was established on 20 September 1940. The name was adapted by Colonel A. T. Lawlor (who was largely responsible for the creation of this unconventional force of yachtsmen, fishermen and others with experience of and a taste for the sea) from *L'Inscription Maritime* raised by Jean Baptiste Colbert, the Finance Minister of Louis XIV, and for a similar purpose, and which numbered amongst its adherents many 'Wild Geese'. The first Maritime Inscription volunteer

98

attested was Pierce M. Purcell, of Dalkey, Co. Dublin. '. . . as regards that night in September 1940', wrote Captain MacKenna, who was present in a junior capacity, 'picture for yourself a great corrugated iron building which was Atlantic Hall—a large body of men of all shapes and sizes in blue dungarees and heavy army boots being drilled in foot drill by Petty Officer the Hon. Patrick Campbell with his famous stutter . . .' On attestation, each volunteer was called out on permanent service and then given indefinite home leave, being liable for recall to duty at any time. Cork's first volunteers were attested on 10 October, and by June 1942 the Maritime Inscription numbered twelve shore companies of 100 men each. On Easter Sunday 1941, the twenty-fifth anniversary of the Rising which was marked by a big parade in Dublin, they appeared for the first time in shore-going rig—also the first time that a naval uniform had been paraded anywhere in the country.

Meanwhile the men who were manning the eighty-eight Look Out Posts maintained by the Coastwatching Service were putting in long, lonely hours in places remote from any habitation for which they were paid the volunteer rate of 2s 6d ($12\frac{1}{2}$p) for a Third Class private (they were under Army control) rising to 3s (15p) a day for a Private First Class. They were granted a special allowance of 3s a day in lieu of rations and accommodation with an additional 2d a day if fuel for the heating of the lookout posts could not be supplied from Army stocks. For this they were required to identify and report on vessels passing within sight of their Post, and in addition to record the movement of aircraft and any communications between ship and shore. Though many of them had to travel long distances to man their posts, it was not found possible to give them a special allocation of bicycle tyres.

'At this stage, before ships reach a premium, before the worst effects of the war at sea are discernible, it might well be desirable for the Government to consider the possibility of inaugurating something in the nature of a state mercantile marine.' William Norton's suggestion, made in the Dáil on 29 September 1939, was revolutionary in its content if not in the manner of its expression. The gross tonnage of ships on the Irish register at the beginning of hostilities was 41,105, a completely unrealistic figure inflated by an Antarctic whaling fleet using an Irish 'address' for whale quota reasons, cross-channel ships owned by British companies and seven large oil tankers in foreign ownership. Following the declaration of war most of these were transferred from the Irish register, leaving fifty-six ships of paltry tonnage and limited by their size to coastal and cross-channel trade. It is worth noting that the tonnage operated by Norway, a similar-sized country, at the time was 4,834,902. These remaining Irish vessels were not even permitted, under British Commonwealth regulations, to sail under their own flag, and the Government's first move was to issue an order replacing the red ensign by the tricolour—an essential step if the neutrality of the diminutive Irish fleet was to be respected. Deputy

Norton's suggestion, however, fell on deaf ears, the Government deciding not to purchase ships until there was no other course open. 'They decided', commented the *Irish Independent*, 'that while neutral ships were available, to charter was better than to send ships with their flag into dangerous waters with all the dangers to neutrality.'

The dangers to neutrality were quickly made apparent, and throughout the Emergency the fleet was subjected to attack on the high seas by both the British and the Germans. In some cases the attacker was not identified, but where evidence was conclusive strong protests were lodged. As de Valera said of the sinking of the *Irish Oak* in the North Atlantic by U-607 on 15 May 1943: 'There was no possibility of mistake. The conditions of visibility were good, and the neutral markings on the ship were perfectly clear. No warning was given, and the first intimation that there was danger was the explosion of the torpedo. We must regard it as an act of Providence that any of the crew was saved.' All the crew was, in fact, picked up by another Irish vessel, *Irish Plane* (Captain D. Henderson) which was fortunately in the vicinity. Both ships belonged to Irish Shipping, a state company which had been set up by the Government in 1941 when it came to the belated conclusion that the country could no longer rely on the ships of other nations to secure its lifelines. Ships at this stage were at a premium, as Deputy Norton had accurately predicted, and it was only with the greatest difficulty that the nucleus of a merchant marine was assembled either by charter or outright purchase. They were a motley collection: *Vassilios Destounis*, 6,100 tons deadweight, built in 1912; *Leda*, 7,250 tons, dating from 1910; the 3,750 ton *Noemi Julia*, 1895, which became the *Irish Hazel*; the Palestinian *Haifa Trader*, 5,300 tons, which sailed under the tricolour as the *Irish Larch*. There were fifteen of them in all, and the largest being the 8,542 ton *Irish Oak*, formerly the *West Neris* and on charter from the United States Government. The most modern was the Danish *Mathilde Maersk*, renamed the *Irish Ash*, which was built in 1921 and joined the Irish Shipping fleet on 27 August 1942. Of these, thirteen survived the war, the other casualty in addition to the *Irish Oak* being the *Irish Pine*—another vessel, formerly the *West Haematite*, on charter from the US—which was sunk with the loss of all hands by U-608 in the North Atlantic on 15 November 1942. She carried a complement of thirty-three.

In April 1942 the dockyard at Rushbrooke, Co. Cork, which had been lying derelict for twelve years, was re-opened for the overhaul of the Irish Shipping fleet, and proved an invaluable asset not only to the State shipping line but to the rest of the merchant marine.

One of the privately-owned vessels to be repaired there in late 1943 was the Wexford Steam Ship Company's *Kerlogue*, a diminutive coaster of 335 gross tons, maximum speed of nine knots, which on 23 October, when 130 miles south of

Ireland, had come under attack from a British plane. 'The ammunition fragments were found to be of British origin', de Valera told the Dáil in December; 'this information was passed to the British Government who instituted an investigation which confirmed that *Kerlogue* had been attacked by a British plane. They informed us the attacking plane did not identify the ship as Irish and that at the time of the attack *Kerlogue* was sailing off course, a fact which has been confirmed from the ship's log.' Irish seamen held several other theories as to the reason for the attack.

*Kerlogue* at the time was on passage to Lisbon via Port Talbot in Wales, a considerable voyage for a little ship of her displacement. Lisbon had become a major transhipment port, and was regularly visited by many Irish ships including the perdurable Arklow schooners. Before leaving the Bristol Channel a ship had to obtain a Navicert from the British naval authorities. 'This document' as Captain Frank Forde explains, 'was designed to control the use of neutral shipping and was a passport to obtain clearance through Allied patrols. Without it a vessel could not receive fuel, water, stores, charts or repair facilities. In the case of the Wexford ships it required them to carry cargo from Britain to the Iberian loading port and to call, homeward bound, to Fishguard, for examination by the Royal Navy.'

Following her repair *Kerlogue* sailed again under Captain Thomas Donohue of Dungarvan and at dawn on 29 December 1943, when homeward bound from Lisbon, she was circled by a German bomber which signalled that help was required. The ship altered course as requested and at 11 a.m. reached the survivors of three German destroyers which had been intercepted and sunk by British cruisers of superior fire-power. 'As rafts rose into view on the crests of giant waves we could see men on them and others clinging to their sides', said *Kerlogue*'s Chief Officer. 'At first we did not know whether they were Allied or Axis until someone noticed the long ribbons trailing downwards from behind a seaman's cap . . .' The coaster picked up 168 survivors, who were crammed into every available space, and ignoring the Navicert regulations which required her to head for Fishguard, Captain Donohue made for Cork. Having radioed ahead for medical assistance he then switched out his apparatus and was thus unable to receive the repeated requests from Land's End Radio to put into Fishguard. Later, in the Welsh port, he had to endure the wrath of a British naval officer who told him that his ship had 'got what she deserved from the RAF a few weeks earlier'.

In all 136 seamen sailing in Irish ships lost their lives in sixteen ships in the Emergency period, and the fleet was responsible for saving 511 men of many nationalities. When the Emergency was over a decoration, known as the Mercantile Marine Service Medal, was issued, to a total of 513, to all who had served a period of six months or over under the Irish flag. The role played by these little ships, most of them plying on routes for which they were never designed and venturing as far afield

as Africa, can scarcely be over-estimated, particularly in the context of a national policy which had steadfastly turned its back on the sea and which, even under Emergency conditions, had been reluctant to face up to the implications of this attitude. On 19 June 1941, Eamon O'Neill, TD, West Cork, asked the Taoiseach to consider the advisability of co-ordinating control of marine services into one Department (the Navy was under the Army, the Mercantile Marine under Industry and Commerce, Sea Fisheries under Agriculture, the Nautical College under Education). 'The existing arrangements', Mr de Valera told him, 'provide for all necessary co-ordination between the Departments concerned.'

On 30 August 1939 four Avro Ansons and two Supermarine Walrus amphibians flew from the Air Corps headquarters at Baldonnel to occupy Rineanna, a vestigial landplane base opposite the flying-boat terminal at Foynes, Co. Limerick. The planes were from the Reconnaissance and Medium Bomber Squadron, under the command of Captain W. J. Keane (an Army rank, since the Air Corps was an integral part of that service). 'Patrols commenced the following day from Lough Swilly along the west and south coasts to Wexford Harbour and were to continue for up to six months', according to A. P. Kearns. 'The patrols lasted for up to three hours each, with great strain on both personnel and aircraft. Rineanna that winter was a god-forsaken place, there was as yet no hanger space to house and maintain aircraft which meant that aircraft had to be sent back to Baldonnel for 20 hour inspection, and whenever major work was required. Eventually training units operated from Rineanna to be followed by some flights of the Fighter Squadron.' Captain Aidan Quigley recalls one such flight: 'We flew frequently as target aircraft for the anti-aircraft batteries ... I was flying up the Dublin coast on a sunny afternoon, accurately maintaining the desired 10,000 feet for the batteries ... as we turned back for the last run along the range I saw a German JU 88 coming in from the east. I knew if he had seen me he would not have gone through the process of closing courteously to identify the markings; a Lysander was a type in common service with the RAF. We quickly sought the refuge of a fat cumulus cloud ...'

Lysanders were one of the more sophisticated types of aircraft flown by the Air Corps in the early Emergency days. Vickers Vespas, Hawker Hinds, Gloster Gladiators (all, in the colloquial phrase, 'wan-engined double wingers') were sound machines in their day, but clearly, with perhaps the exception of the Gladiators, no match for Spitfires and Messerschmit 109s. The problem was the usual one. 'I asked for a list of armaments ordered from Great Britain, number of aeroplanes, etc.' General Mulcahy noted with reference to a meeting of the Defence Conference in late 1940. 'On Wednesday 20th Traynor, to show how difficult it was to do this, brought over, in the shape of a big file, a copy of an order for aeroplanes and parts. Seven Anson aeroplanes were on the list ... When I asked how many aeroplanes were on order, he could not say ...' One method of supply was to salvage crashed aircraft, which totalled some 170 from all sources (i.e. Britain, Germany and the United States) in the Emergency period. German aircraft were usually conscientiously destroyed by their crew-members, in the event of any of them surviving the crash, but this policy was not generally adopted by the Allies. On 29 January Mulcahy noted that Aiken had informed the Defence Conference that they had tried to put into service a Spitfire which had force-landed, but could not procure a replacement propeller and other parts.

The civil arm fared a little better. Aer Lingus had inaugurated its services in 1936 with a De Haviland Dragon, and in April 1940 it acquired its first Douglas DC3. The aircraft had been delivered to Antwerp from America, and it was flown out of the Belgian airport by an Aer Lingus pilot just ahead of the invading Germans. One of its early duties was to carry a distinguished assembly of Government Ministers, service chiefs and Aer Lingus directors on an aerial inspection of what was still being called 'Shannon Air Base'. Thenceforth the company maintained a regular international service in conjunction with the British West Coast Air Services Ltd, flying either to Liverpool or Manchester as war conditions permitted. It also serviced the route between Dublin, where the new Collinstown airport terminal was opened in 1941, and Rineanna, which was also the terminus for 'VIP' flights from Britain to connect with the transatlantic flying-boat services. The fare was £5.50 return. Foynes had become the eastern terminal on 6 September 1939, when Pan-American curtailed its routes to Southampton and Marseilles. The flights were restarted after a break in May 1942, and in October 1943 Brendan O'Regan took over from the British Overseas Airways Corporation the responsibility for catering at the base, thus laying the foundation of the Shannon Sales and Catering Organisation and the future international airport. William Sheridan, the first chef at the Foynes terminal, is credited with the distinction of inventing the confection subsequently to become universally known as Irish Coffee.

Even though the Air Corps later acquired from Britain Miles Magister trainers and a number of Hawker Hurricane fighters, it lacked Radar and other ground support and was never in a strong position to intercept and force down aircraft which violated Irish air space. In some cases it did not even try. Sunderlands and Catalinas from bases in Northern Ireland were permitted to fly out over Bundoran on patrols instead of being obliged to keep clear of the north Donegal coastline, and Allied aircraft which made forced landings whilst on 'non-operational flights', a category that was susceptible to generous interpretation, were permitted to repair any damage and return to their bases. German arrivals on the other hand, remained for good, and usually in the form of useless fragments. There was a dump for such salvaged remains at Baldonnel.

One German plane, however, arrived very much in one piece—a JU88G6 night fighter which took off from an airfield in Denmark on 5 May 1945 as the war was in its dying stages and landed at 5.15 a.m. at Gormanstown. 'The crew switched the engines off and clambered out of the aeroplane', recalls Captain Quigley, who was present at the time. 'They were wearing Luftwaffe uniforms with the ugly bum freezer jackets. The pilot, a sergeant major, had facial scars; blue eyed and blond, he looked a tough customer and he wore the Iron Cross . . . the German explained to the commandant that Denmark had surrendered, and that his squadron had been given the choice by their commander of flying their machines to neutral countries before the truce was valid. He had decided to come to Ireland, and he recounted, with just a twinkle of Teutonic humour, how he had flown all the way across England, flat out and very low, gun button safetied, and admired the scenery for the first time.' The British repaid him by coming over to collect his aircraft for examination on the following 1 June, apparently finding its equipment of considerable interest.

As the war neared its end there was extensive speculation as to the role Ireland would play in peacetime international aviation. 'During a recent period of twelve months', Seán Lemass told the Dáil in March 1944, 'the average monthly number of persons arriving at and departing from Shannon Airport (Foynes) by air were 666 and 678 respectively . . . There are 109 persons of whom 107 are Irish citizens employed by the State on aviation services . . . It is understood that the staffs employed at Foynes by operating companies total 220 . . .' Here, clearly, was the nucleus of something big, and it was with this in mind that the Government signed the Interim Agreement and Convention on Civil Aviation in Chicago on 12 December of the same year. 'International air transport air operators, in the present stage of aeronautical development', Lemass said in the following April, 'have a major interest in obtaining transit and non-traffic rights in this country because of our geographical position and our importance to operators over the Atlantic route, the route which, it is confidently expected, will be the blue ribbon route of air transport. While our participation in air transport operation over the Atlantic is contemplated at some stage, we have not at present the same degree of interest in advancing our rights as operators as we have in establishing our interests as air transport facility providers and in considering the signature of the two documents the paramount factor was the effect of our action on the future of Shannon Airport.'

James Dillon agreed that Shannon had a future, but for freight only, on the model of the entrepôt of Danzig. 'We have no more chance of collecting the transatlantic passenger traffic', he said, 'than we have of making emus breed in Kerry . . .'

NO CIGARETTES

# *Interlude: an bhfuil an 'medium' agat?*

*After twenty years of effort, the culture of Ireland is still overwhelmingly Anglo-Saxon, nakedly or in word for word translation.*

HUBERT BUTLER, 1941

*If, and as long as everyone, or practically everyone, learns English, British culture and British ideas will acquire an increasingly stronger grip here. To restore Irish is not enough: it is also necessary to banish English.*

The Leader, 1942

I N  T H E  face of it the isolation of the Emergency years should have provided the ideal opportunity for the Irish language to come into its own; the means were to hand, and precedents were not lacking. 'In Oslo he had witnessed the rebirth of the old Norwegian language against the still current Danish of the former Danish domination', said Kees Van Hoek of Dr Edouard Hempel. 'In Dublin he was to witness the strides of Irish against English, a much harder battle, but one of strong similarities.' It would, indeed, have been a much harder battle, had it ever been joined. But, for reasons which lie largely outside the historical scope of the present narrative, the challenge was not generally accepted, and the status of Irish in May 1945 was very little altered from what it had been in September 1939.

In December of the latter year Earnán de Blaghd wrote: 'There is practically nothing to read in Irish. People who want bi-lingualism and whose idea is that Irish should merely be something in the nature of a quaint survival in the National Life may be satisfied with the achievements of the Gúm ... but its 483 titles in the general literature class represent a very inconsiderable contribution towards the furnishing of an Irish Library ...' Official policy with regard to the language had not noticeably altered in the years since the establishment of the State, and whilst the language remained compulsory for children there was little or no attempt made to interest the non-committed adult in continuing to use it once he had emerged from the educational machine. And the committed did little to assist in the matter. 'We feel absolutely certain', wrote *The Leader* in November 1939, 'that nothing could be more calculated to put the younger generation off the reading of Irish than for them to see practically nothing discussed in Irish but Irish itself and the saving of Irish.' It seemed, indeed, that the language movement was engaged in consuming its own tail, with the inevitable consequence, and the outlook was not brightened, in *The Leader*'s view, by Mr de Valera's assumption of the office of Minister for Education in addition to his other onerous duties. 'The danger about Mr de Valera as Minister for Education', it wrote, 'is that while his interest in Irish is real and sincere, his ideas about methods and measures are entirely out of date ... in language matters he is a well-meaning Rip Van Winkle who with a good heart may do an infinity of damage.' In the event his sins were more those of omission than commission, as apart from some juggling with class readers he contented himself for the most part in rendering lip-service to the ideal. 'If a proper wholehearted effort be made at once', he told the Ard Craobh of the Gaelic League in 1942, 'I feel certain that the language can be restored, but if we rely on half-measures and the majority of the people remain apathetic, notwithstanding what has been done, the language will inevitably disappear as a spoken language.'

The half-measures remained in force and the majority of the people reacted as the Taoiseach had predicted. One body, Radio Eireann, which was making a serious attempt to promote the language, was particularly affected by the general apathy. 'The Irish side of the programmes suffered from two lasting shortages', said Maurice Gorham, subsequently director of the broadcasting service, '—of material and of reaction from the audience. Séamus O Braonáin, himself an enthusiastic Irish speaker, has recorded the difficulty of getting a reasonable supply of suitable matter in Irish and even a fair supply of talkers and actors who were definitely suitable ... Coupled with this was the complete silence from the audience, except for one or two regular correspondents ... Programmes could be very good, indifferent, or bad, he said; all were received in silence.'

A silence of similar density pervaded the Dáil when matters relating to the language revival were referred to, Deputies contenting themselves for the most part with the making of the token gesture that had become habitual and the asking of the customary nit-picking questions. On 27 October 1943 Mr Seán McEntee informed the house that six County Managers possessed a sufficient competency in Irish to enable them to discharge their duties efficiently through the medium; three had a good knowledge and eleven 'a knowledge which is less than good'. In the Financial Year 1942-3, the cost of the revival of the language was estimated at £319,993, a figure which included £400 for the translation of the New Testament; £2,400 for publication of secondary school books; and £458 in salary for the translator of military manuals.

The latter figure was doubtless well earned, for both the regular and emergency volunteer forces maintained Irish-speaking units, and here at least a real enthusiasm for the language, born, no doubt out of its application to day-to-day practicalities, was made manifest. Attempts to extend its use, however, to less dedicated formations met with some setbacks. As Patrick Campbell puts it: 'After a couple of weeks being drilled in English the NCO in charge of us suddenly said: "From now on youse bowsies'll be doing it in Irish". There was a roar of outraged complaint. "Sure we can't even do it in muckin' English yet", was the burden of it, and many of us couldn't, indeed.

'The next couple of weeks were plain chaos. The NCO would bawl at us something that sounded like "Mel-arrah!" and we'd stand there glaring back at him, having no idea of what to do. There'd be a stream of querulous complaint—"What's the muckin' eejit on about at all?" and then some of us would experimentally come to attention, followed gradually by the rest. The next order sounded like "Go mere-marshawl!" Some of us marked time, others turned to the right, while the largest group went back to standing at ease.'

Civilians, too, found the language a mixed blessing. The Daly family of Mullingar, having been erroneously informed that extra rations could be obtained by registering for ration books in Irish, discovered that no retailer in the town would honour them, and spent six months living on the charity of others until the offending documents were replaced by their equivalent in the country's second language. As Piaras Beaslaí put it in a more general context: 'Nothing seems to change very much in the Irish Language Movement since it first became an important force in the country's life. The problems of thirty or forty years ago are still the problems of today. A new generation is carrying on the old controversies, and repeating the same arguments in much the same words. In an Ireland that has seen such great changes, in a world of chaotic impermanence, this persistence of attitudes is a curious spectacle.'

It would be wrong to give the impression, however, that there was no movement for change. If official policies seemed frozen, there was ample scope for individual effort and literature in Irish, indeed, seemed to be thriving in adversity. Mairtín O Cadhain established 'Gaeltachts' in the Curragh camp and there laid the foundations of his own major work; Mairtin O Direán's *Coinnle Geala* appeared in 1942; Seosamh Mac Grianna's *Mo Bealach Féin* in 1940. In spite of the paper shortage there was an irruption of periodical literature: *An Glór, Comhar, Inniu, Ar Aghaidh*. A movement within the Gaelic League led to the establishment of a ginger group, Craobh na hAiseirghe, which later split into cultural and political wings, Glún na Buaidhe and Ailtirí na hAiseirghe respectively. A proposed publication by the latter, which was of markedly right-wing tendency, was refused a paper quota in 1944. Plans for the publication of *Eire: A Gaelic Golden Treasury* were announced in September 1939. 'Commentaries in foreign languages, hitherto unpublished pictures, and a section in which industrial and commercial products of all kinds are advertised in Irish, are some of the unusual and attractive features ...' wrote *The Leader*. 'Never before has the scope and strength of the Gaelic revival been so revealed, and many will be astonished at the huge field in which its influence is now evident.'

'Irish has an intrinsic significance', said Myles na gCopaleen, 'which (naturally enough), must be unknown to those who condemn the language' (he was responding to an attack on the revival movement by the editor of his own paper). 'It provides through its literature and dialects a great field for the pursuit of problems philological, historical and ethnological, an activity agreeable to all men of education and goodwill.' One form which this pursuit had taken was the attempt to make the language more accessible to the residents of the Galltacht by simplifying the spelling and smoothing out the dialectal differences—two projects guaranteed to bring down the wrath of the purists. Opposition was not, however, confined to professional philologists: a letter from 'Dublin Gael' in the *Irish Independent* of 1 June 1941 took two of the reformers sternly to task. 'The Litriu Simpli of Dr Bergin and Shan O Cuiv (er yes De gu roiv a anam) has a few supporters,' it stated, 'though I imagine its chances are slender ... The best and most practical form of the Irish dialects put forward is Eirish ... Eirish looks more easy, organic and balanced than any other form. The following examples well illustrate the difference between Gaedhlige, Litriu Simpli and Eirish:

> An arán laetheamhail tabhair dhúinn indiú
> Ar n-arán Lähuil túir Úing iniuv
> Ar aran laaga tug do-in iniu'

Piaras Beaslaí adopted a different approach. 'I have come to the conclusion', he said, 'that what is urgently needed is a form of "Basic Irish" and text-books written in this basic tongue, for the use of elementary students of Irish . . . a committee of three sane and commonsensible Gaelic scholars (if such Gaelic scholars can be found) should be able to decide on the absolutely essential words and phrases . . .' The proposition provoked a good deal of attention, and *Passing Variety* was moved to contribute its own measure of essential Irish suitable to the times and conditions prevailing:

'1. Do dhéin sé carabhat capail as: he made a horses's collar out of it.
2. Tá sé in a malaí aosta: He's an oul' bags.
3. Cá raibh tu sa mbliain 1014?: Where were you in 1014?
4. An bhfuil an 'Medium' agat?: Do you speak Irish?
5. An bhfuil tú in san Stát Seirbhise?: Are you up from the country?
6. Tá tú ag dul do dtí Pairc an Shelbourne: You are going to the dogs.
7. Tá ac agam: I have a butt.
8. Is mór an truagh é: Oh the pity of it all.'

Others feared that modernisation could go too far. 'A certain use of foreign words is permissible in any language', said *The Leader*, 'but carried too far it must bring the language gradually into contempt', and offered the following example:

'Leig an t-aeroplane bomb anuas an Town Hall agus chuir na daoine a gcuid gas-masks ortha féin agus d'fán siad sa' shelter nó gur chualadar an all-clear signal'. Myles na gCopaleen carried this kind of thing to its illogical conclusion, if in the opposite direction: 'Aigh nó a mean thú ios so Lésaigh dat thí slíps in this clós, bhéars a bíord, and dos not smóc bíocós obh de trobal obh strageing a meaits. It is só long sins thí did an asasth dea's bhorc dat thí thincs 'manuil leabear' is do neim obh a Portuguis arditeitear.'

In 1943 the Minister for Posts and Telegraphs, Patrick Little, suggested that in its broadcasts in Irish Radio Eireann should proceed as if the language were the vernacular of the whole country. Even in the Gaeltacht this was a scarcely tenable proposition; of the 5,134 legal cases heard in North Donegal between 1 August 1939 and 31 May 1941 only 824 were heard wholly in Irish; the comparable figures for West Galway were 5,101 out of a total of 10,065. The assumption was, however, enshrined in the title of Radio Eireann's new series *Is Your Irish Rusty?* with its implication that all that most people required was a short refresher course to restore them to absolute fluency. In March 1945, though, the nettle was grasped more firmly, when Aindrias O Muimhneacháin launched another programme under the more straightforward title of *Listen and Learn*. The simultaneous publication of booklets to accompany the course, something of an innovation at the time, ensured its popularity and the series ran eventually for ten years.

'There is no basis at all for the theory that a people cannot preserve a separate national entity without a distinct language', said Myles, uttering what was then accounted as a major heresy in most revivalist circles, 'but it is beyond dispute that Irish enshrines the national ethos . . . In advocating the preservation of Irish culture, it is not to be inferred *that this culture* is superior to the English or any other but simply that certain Irish modes are *more comfortable and suitable* for Irish people . . .'

Had all the proposals been as modest, the story might have been different.

" What did you think of Ireland ? "
" I loved the Lakes of Killarney and the steak an' onions."

# From war to peace in one hour twelve minutes

*Dublin was full of interesting refugees from London. The Shelbourne Hotel was alive with people trying to rent houses and fiddle their Bentleys aboard the B & I boat in Liverpool.*

PATRICK CAMPBELL

*The sequestration of Ireland created, for the Shelbourne, conditions very unlike those of the First World War. Hungry British journalists, as happy to be in Dublin as their forbears had been displeased, headed upon arrival for the hotel; first to eat, then to type gargantuan stories of Irish eating for the papers they happened to represent. Mystery men with sealed lips and locked brief-cases shot through the hall and up and down in the lift.*

ELIZABETH BOWEN

*There was no sensation of going to an ideologically-distinct country. It was as if the Allies had voluntarily set apart a region where steaks and drink and bright lights were provided; a kind of convalescent home.*

BRIAN INGLIS

ED MURROW, the American radio correspondent, made the seventy-two
minute flight from Britain to Ireland in January 1941. He found that the Dublin
theatres were flourishing and the talk was sparkling, but was refused admission
to a dance because he was not wearing a black tie. This slight contretempts apart, his
experience was that of most of the refugees, permanent and temporary, from wartime
Britain: incredulity that a country so close to the war zone could, on the surface at
least and in the levels of society to which he was introduced, be so little affected by
the holocaust. 'The Irish populace is shockingly ignorant of the war and the issues at
stake', thundered the British *War Illustrated* early in 1942; there is 'universal
ignorance of what is going on', complained the London *Daily Telegraph* in July of
the same year. 'If the Irish insist on becoming another Belgium probably no
Power—even the US, can do anything about it', the *Aeroplane* magazine, straying
somewhat from its accustomed field, had concluded some months earlier. The
Americans were, at the beginning at least, of two minds whether they should even try
to do anything; in November 1940, 2,500 people attended a meeting in New York
which established the 'American Friends of Irish Neutrality'. But President
Roosevelt was not one of them. 'Would Irish freedom be permitted as an amazing
exception in an unfree world?' he asked rhetorically in a radio broadcast the
following month. 'Thousands and thousands of American soldiers will die because of
the Irish position', protested the *Atlanta Constitution*. 'As long as the neutrality of
Switzerland, Sweden, or Spain is not attributed to ignorance or indifference one
must be at a loss to know why Ireland should be held up among so many as the one
country which is neutral for immoral reasons', complained *The Bell*.

The moral issue, to which Mr de Valera, the Irish government and the Irish
people had been blind, in the view of the Professor Commager, writing in the *New
York Times Magazine*, was something which the influx of refugees from the war
could well put on one side. 'There was a party somewhere in Dublin every night',
recalls Patrick Campbell. 'The English refugees lined up the bottles and we brought
our friends along to drink them ... We knew the interesting pubs. We knew the
owners and trainers and the jockeys. We were able to show the English a better time
than they could have found for themselves. And every day more were arriving so that
we could reject the dull ones, and choose the most amusing—and the most
generous.'

Not all those arriving were in this fun-loving category. Clearing centres had to
be set up to deal with deported IRA members and sympathisers in 1940, and
amongst those arriving at Rosslare in the early days were many children. ('It's
terrible for all those English children being "vacuated"', said a little Dublin girl as
reported by Quidnunc in the *Irish Times*. 'Why?' asked a friend. 'I had it done and it
hurt my arm terrible.') For most, however, the transition from war to neutrality was

relatively painless. 'The moment came', wrote Elizabeth Bowen, 'when those crowded on deck, dropping their life-belts, beheld the lights of Ireland under the fading outline of the hills, and watched these lamps and windows enlarge, brighten as the ship, the throb of her engines silenced, to the sound of a long rushing from the water, drew alongside the pier. After the black-out left behind in England, Dublin herself seemed as dazzling, legendary as New York.'

Apart from those wartime immigrants whose main concern was protecting their investments and their skins, there were those who were protecting their ideals. Ireland played temporary host to a number of artists and writers for whom it represented something more than just a non-involved country: 'To live in Ireland at a time when the world around us is convulsed and harrowed by hate, bitterness and distrust', wrote Kees Van Hoek, 'is a spiritual tonic. Ages old as a nation, politically young as a state, Ireland has preserved an essential sanity'. Some of these refugees were, in the words of Margot Moffett, 'imports of real wealth'—people, perhaps, like the painter Nick Nicholls, who published a poem *The Bone and the Flower*, which stirred up controversy in *The Bell* and was included in a post-Emergency anthology of contemporary Irish poetry. Others were of less sterling worth, and whilst the natives could accept the simple logic of a man leaving Britain for hard financial reasons, their attitude to those professing other ideals remained cautiously enigmatic. 'Is the Minister aware', asked J. McCann, TD in the Dáil on 17 February 1943, 'that there are certain musicians coming into this country evading service in their own country who, I understand, will be applicants for these posts? (He was referring to 12 vacancies in the Radio Eireann Orchestra, for which 125 applications had been received.) Surely the Minister will not consider giving posts to any of these people?' Happily for the future of Irish music, the Minister did so consider. R. B. D. French, in his imaginary evocation of Christmas 1941 amongst the landed gentry, echoes, though in a very different manner, the same underlying attitude. The scene is the Shelbourne Hotel, late afternoon:

'A large party? Heavens no, my dear, there wasn't a soul except ourselves, except that at the last minute Gerald and I decided to bring Alastair along. Oh, yes, you *do*! Rather pale and tall, with corduroy trousers and a beard. You must have seen him in the Buttery or the Country Shop or somewhere. *Do*? Why, my poor poppet, surely you've read *How Slim was my Volume* and *Main Drain*? But you *must*! Simply superb, and such *malignance* having the police seizing them in England even before they were banned here. Well, the poor pet was absolutely *lost* over Christmas with everybody away, and of course he couldn't go back to England because of military service and all that, so we took him along, and do you know I had the feeling that Betty and Jack were quite surprised? ...

'However, Christmas Eve was quite fun. You see, we knew Betty and Jack would be simply agog to see Alistair's private film *Le Chef de Gare*. (You haven't? My dear, it simply begins where *La Femme du Boulanger* leaves off.) So we fixed up a sheet in the dining-room while Betty and Jack were telephoning to the Rector to say they couldn't go to the carol service. But in the end we couldn't show it after all because of the fuses fusing ... so then we all went into Cloughjordan in the car to get candles. (Between ourselves, we thought it rather lucky, because Betty and Jack used up all their petrol, which meant that we shouldn't have to go to church in the morning—though of course we didn't say so to *them*!)

'On the way back Gerald made us stop at the local and gave us drinks. Do you know, Betty and Jack had never been in the village pub in their *lives*, and were quite unwilling to go in—just because they might meet the yard boy and some of their farm people! Did you ever *hear* of such stickiness? But, as I said, at Christmas time we're all just one big family together—don't you agree?—and Alastair soon had us all singing Breton carols. (Well he and I did anyway). But they really don't seem to *know* about parties in the country, and quite soon the village people said they had to go, so we all went home.'

The protective chauvinism of Betty and Jack was a not uncommon reaction; it was invoked also in the case of more purposeful visitors from the outside world, at least some of whom were patently hostile. 'Since the beginning of the war', Frank Aiken told the Dáil in 1944, 'a number of foreign newspapers have tried to bedevil the relations between Ireland and England and between Ireland and the United States of America ... In order to stop one word from borrowing another and to prevent our people losing their balanced judgement by the publication in our papers of unfair attacks by individual trouble-making foreign journalists, I have prohibited, consistently, since the beginning of the war, the publication in our papers of these attacks, except in the case where definite allegations were made which had to be countered in the national interests by authoritative statements ...' He was referring specifically to a story transmitted by Associated Press that the Irish Red Cross had invited Axis representatives to a Ceilidhe in Dublin Castle but had failed to invite the American Minister. A US film company making a *March of Time* film on 'Neutral Ireland' came under similar fire, this time for faking shots at a social function. The Dáil was not pacified by Aiken's explanation that they had also been filming 'Army, Marine Service, ARP and fire-fighting exercises, Maynooth College, the GAA finals, the Oireachtas Reception, the export of livestock, the shipping of bloodstock to Spain and Portugal ...'

In the case of any visit which might lead to a compromising of the state of neutrality the Government reacted sharply. The incident of Dr Jan Masaryk is a case in point. Dr Masaryk, the Minister for Foreign Affairs of the Republic of Czechslovakia (in exile) visited Dublin at the beginning of November 1944 and

spoke at a meeting in Trinity College, the Taoiseach, Mr de Valera, being also on the platform. The Government then discovered that he had been invited to address a private meeting of the Irish Institute for International Affairs on the afternoon of Friday 3rd. A harmless-looking enough engagement, but the Institute, which was set up in 1936 on the model of the similarly-named British Institute, an organisation which was virtually a mouthpiece for official Foreign Office policies and attitudes, was, in leadership, of markedly pro-Allied sympathies. The 'leading lights . . . these four or five gentlemen who put themselves above the Government' in de Valera's words, were Senator Douglas, Donal O'Sullivan, James J. Auchmuty and J. T. O'Farrell. 'It is well that the facts about this so-called Irish Institute of International Affairs should be known', the Taoiseach told the Dáil. 'First of all, it is not a chartered body. It has no kind of official recognition or approval. Indeed, it has no legal existence whatsoever, and the title Irish Institute of International Affairs is simply self-assumed . . . I am satisfied beyond doubt, from the information at my disposal . . . that the Irish Institute has become a focus of propaganda devoted entirely to furthering and encouraging a particular point of view in relation to the present war.' He answered previous criticisms from the Institute that the Government refused the right of anyone to study international affairs except themselves. 'That statement is false in every particular. The more interest people take in external affairs the better we like it. What we object to is the misuse of an organisation and a name to endeavour to bring the Government of its own country into contempt and to create embarrassment for it in external relations.' De Valera, who himself held the portfolio of External Affairs, did permit himself to state that: 'we have the greatest possible respect for Dr Masaryk in this country', but if the incident appears as something of a storm in a teacup it is typical of the sensitivity with which the Government, and particularly the Taoiseach, reacted to any threat, real or imaginary, to the integrity of Ireland's neutral status.

'Even in the black year of 1940', wrote Patrick Campbell, 'the war really didn't seem to have much to do with us. There was no public opinion to shame young men into joining up. It seemed perfectly normal to be neutral.' Some however, were shamed, if not by public opinion, by the rooted loyalties of their families into serving the Allied cause. Others followed them for a variety of reasons, but whatever the motivation, their subsequent activities overseas are outside the scope of the present enquiry. They came and went on leave, as did also those who were serving the British war effort in civilian capacities. Some of the latter, returning after spending Christmas in Ireland, had clothing, underwear and shoes confiscated by the Revenue authorities at Rosslare, even though claiming the articles were their personal property; the State's attitude to both its civilian and professional mercenaries was nothing if not ambivalent. So, of course, were the attitudes of those who had elected for that course of action: Brian Inglis, on flying training in Rhodesia, heard a rumour that Britain had invaded Ireland. He and an Irish colleague had decided to present themselves for internment when the rumour was scotched.

For those serving with the British the situation in Dublin possessed its special piquancy. 'There was even one occasion during the war', Inglis said 'when I took a drink with Smyllie and the German Press attaché in Dublin, who had the engagingly loaded name of Karl Petersen ... To have exchanged casual pub conversation with the citizen of a country which I was engaged in fighting would, I thought, make a good story to tell when I got back to the mess ...'

On 25 January 1945 there were resident in the country 479 aliens who had registered under the Aliens Order. 123 of those were United States citizens, mostly of Irish birth or descent. Of the others (British and British Commonwealth citizens were not considered as Aliens) ten were engaged in business, trade or agriculture other than as employees. The most significant group however, were those who did not appear on the Aliens' Register: the diplomatic corps which continued to represent both belligerent and neutral nations and which was the greatest single cause of adverse comment from abroad once the agitation for the handing over of the Treaty ports had died down. These criticisms were directed, by Allied interests, at the continuing presence in Dublin of representatives of Germany, Italy and Japan and are considered elsewhere (p. 131). Here, it is the composition of this tight little group, several of them virtually marooned in Ireland by the fortunes of war, which is of interest. The Belgian Minister, M. Maurice Goor, decided to remain permanently in Ireland, because, as he put it, 'I loathe snobbery and so do the Irish. They are always their natural selves.' It was the 'human simplicity' of the Irish which appealed most to Edouard Hempel, the German Minister. The Canadian High Commissioner, John Doherty Kearney, who played a valuable role in mediating between Dublin and Washington at the time of the crisis over the American Note, was the son of a Co. Louth father and a Co. Tyrone mother and was married to a Cork woman. His Official Secretary was Ed. Garland, an Irish emigrant, and his private secretary, Edith O'Malley, was of Connemara ancestry. The origins of his strong sympathy with Ireland's position are thus not hard to trace. The Italian Minister, Signor Vicenzo Berardis, was supported by an Italian Irish colony of some 400, of whom two of the most prominent were Dr Tomacelli of Trinity College and Professor Morozzo Della Rocca of University College, Cork; other diplomats, such as General Franco's representative, Señor Don Juan García-Ontiveras y Laplana, had virtually no responsibilities in this direction, there being no more than two or three Spaniards in the country. The Axis representatives apart, the two diplomats who created most interest and aroused the greatest controversy were those of Great Britain and the United States: Sir John Maffey and David Gray.

At the outbreak of war Britain had no diplomatic representative in Ireland, though an Irish High Commissioner had been accredited to London. The impediments were, of course, constitutional, the British shrinking from the explicit recognition of Ireland's republican status which the appointment of a full diplomatic mission would involve. Maffey was thus known as the 'British Representative to Eire' (the British had preferred the preposition 'in'; the amendment was de Valera's) and his headquarters at 50 Upper Mount Street was described as an office rather than a chancellery. 'He is not a High Commissioner', said the Parisian *Le Temps*, 'for that would imply that Ireland recognised the Commonwealth. Nor is he strictly an Ambassador because that would mean that England recognised the Irish Republic. He is solely the Representative of Great Britain in Ireland with diplomatic status.' Maffey's background was that of colonial rectitude; he had served in India and had spent the years 1925–32 as Governor-General of the Anglo-Egyptian Sudan. 'He visited Abyssinia', the *Irish Independent* recorded in an interview, 'where his respect for Italian colonial endeavour was genuine.'

Maffey adopted what would in contemporary cant be described as a 'low profile'; not so David Gray, the United States Minister. De Valera, in a moment of unusual candour, told General Mulcahy in May 1941 that only for the very delicate situation, and the fact that Gray's wife was a relative of Roosevelt, he would have asked his Government to recall him. Mrs Gray was in fact the aunt of the President's wife. The Minister had been an admirer of de Valera's policies during a year he had spent in Castletownsend, Co. Cork, writing a book on Ireland that was never to be finished, but this attitude underwent a marked change in the time he spent as his country's representative in Dublin. 'A man of great charm and manner and a keen sense of humour', the *Irish Times* said of him on his arrival in April 1940. 'There is little, if any, trace of American accent in his speech'. His big American car with the Florida plates tended to gravitate towards the houses occupied by the remnants of the Ascendancy. His growing detestation of Ireland's neutrality and of the personality of its chief protagonist reached a culmination in the affair of the American Note (see page 138). 'It was in fact extremely difficult for reasonable men to believe that the head of a small and powerless State could assume the lunatic arrogance which at times is characteristic of Mr de Valera', he wrote to Roosevelt in 1944. It is only fair to add that Maffey's attitude differed at times only in degree: 'He (de Valera) is the physical and mental expression of the most narrow-minded and bigoted section of the country ...' he said. Since the continuing purpose of both gentlemen was to pursuade, bully or cajole Ireland into abandoning its neutrality in their favour their attitudes are not entirely surprising, but Gray evinced a degree of bitterness and personal spite which in the end proved a source of some embarrassment.

For most members of the diplomatic corps, however, particularly those such as the Polish Chargé d'Affaires, who had no effective government to represent, or even for the much-travelled French Minister, Xavier de Laforcade, life in neutral Ireland was both agreeable and undemanding. Some of the corps lived in some magnificence, as in the case of the Italian Minister in Luttrelstown Castle, Clonsilla. The French maintained an elegant legation in Ailesbury Road; Herr Hempel occupied the house of the former, and final, Governor General, Liam O Buachalla, in Monkstown near Dun Laoghaire, where he found time to pursue his linguistic and literary interests.

'Eire's neutrality is a real danger to the Allied cause', the *Pocket Guide to Northern Ireland* informed United States servicemen destined for temporary residence in the province: 'There, just across the channel from embattled England, and not too far from your own billets in Ulster, the Axis nations maintain large legations and staffs. These Axis agents send out weather reports, find out by espionage what is going on in Ulster ...'

These putative activities did not deter Ulster citizens from descending on Dublin and other southern towns and cities whenever the opportunity offered, actively encouraged by the Irish Tourist Association. 'A very major part of the Shelbourne's intake, however, during this strange time was from the Six Counties', wrote Elizabeth Bowen. 'Ulster's participation in the war-effort, under the Union Jack, kept her workshops, docks and factories humming ... South, therefore, over the Border streamed Northerners, jingling money wherewith to eat, drink and buy ...' And the temptation to return with tangible evidence of such Lucullan living was irresistible. Smuggling developed into a major industry, smuggling in both directions, since such items as, for example, bicycle parts and accessories were virtually unobtainable in Eire whilst being available, if in modest quantities, in the North. Des Mooney, 'criminal and hardware merchant' in Leland Bardwell's *Girl on a Bicycle* is a typical, if fictional, representative of the smuggling fraternity:

'I came looking for you Saturday night.'

'I was over the border.'

'I guessed.'

'Dunwoody, the customs officer, has gone for his tea.'

'Will he talk?'

'Fuckin' eejit. Still there's nothing they can pin on me. Nah. Uncle Des is too clever by half.'

'What is it this time?'

'Same old thing. Bicycle tubes, wheels, spares—but it can all be shipped to Dublin at the drop of a hat.'

'Following the depression due to the falling off in cattle smuggling,' *Dublin Opinion* advised in November 1940, 'things have brightened up on the Border again, and the onion smuggler has come into his own.' Two Dundalk men attempted to introduce five tons of this vegetable illegally into the Six Counties by removing the wagons in which they were being transported from the train to which they were attached whilst it was held for customs examination, and subsequently re-attaching them: an example of dexterity which was perhaps deserving of a better fate. The railway lines, operated on British-supplied coal by the GNR, which crossed the Border, were, of course, favourite smuggling routes. Some of these, such as the Dundalk–Enniskillen and Clones–Belfast, crossed and recrossed the frontier in a manner which was the despair of the customs authorities and the delight of the smugglers, who became so ingenious at concealing contraband that wire netting was stretched across spaces under the seats and over ventilators. Venerable coaches with spartan wooden seats, borrowed from the Great Southern, were also introduced to discourage the enterprising traveller. On the Dublin–Belfast route, which continued to boast a dining car, it was not unknown for items of jewellery to be dropped thoughtfully into glasses of stout as the train approached the Border by orotund ladies clad in several layers of newly-acquired garments (this was, of course, before clothes rationing in Eire). The railway authorities were finally obliged to suspend meal and drink services between the Southern and Northern customs stations, Dundalk and Goraghwood.

The Ulster visitors received a warm welcome, and not only for commercial reasons. There was a strong sympathy for the danger and deprivations they were enduring, as evidenced by de Valera's dispatch of the Dublin fire brigades northwards at the time of the 1941 Belfast bombings, at some considerable risk to his neutrality policy; and, in the case of one Dublin hotel at least, this indulgence was extended to any of the few travellers who filtered through. 'It was the rooted belief of all the Shelbourne chambermaids', says Elizabeth Bowen, 'that those arriving from London were to be treated as casualties from bomb-shock: voices and footsteps were accordingly muted, soft ministrations were many, and in no night-nursery could one have been more fondly, soothingly tucked up in bed ...'

# A pedicure business in the South Mall

*Although I had nowhere abroad found better friends than in Ireland, I have sometimes had the feeling that I might perhaps have carried out my task better if I had by chance been born a Catholic. I felt there was a corner in their hearts to which I had no access and which could not be opened to me.*                                CAPT. HERMAN GÖRTZ

*Basically, the population is a mixture of Western and Nordic components. Characteristics are the lively temperament, good nature, gaiety, eagerness for music and dancing, instruction and social entertainment. The Irishman depends upon a community built upon the equality of all, but joins to it an extraordinary personal need of independence which easily degenerates into a lack of discipline and quarrelsomeness and makes larger political power-formation difficult.*

Militär Geographische Ausgaben über Irland

SPIES ARE like fleas: find one and you start itching everywhere. 'Galway being used as a U-boat base', accused the *Washington Evening Star* in November 1940. 'German spies, I was assured on many an occasion, abounded in Eire', Brian Inglis recalled; 'certain Dublin bars were full of them, and at night

27. On the barricades: the LDF in action.

28.  Mobilisation: Army motor cyclists prepare to move off.

29.  The sedate pace of an Emergency funeral.

30.  Acting suspiciously: a road patrol takes no chances.

31. Howth Castle and Environs: Howth Branch, LDF.

32. First blood: crater at Campile, Co. Wexford.

33. "Carlow Ford": now thrive the armourers.

34. Remembering how they stood: De Valera and
Government colleagues at 1916 Commemoration parade,
Easter 1941.

U-boats were regularly surfacing off the west coast to land arms and agents, and to take on fuel . . .' 'We had Intelligence reports that an unidentified ship which might have been a submarine tender had been seen off the coast', said Captain Fell of the British decoy ship *Tamura*. 'There seems to be a good deal of evidence, or at any rate suspicion, that the U-boats are being succoured from West of Ireland ports by the malignant section with whom de Valera dare not interfere' said Winston Churchill in late September 1939. 'The charges were improbable, especially the re-fuelling of U-boats', Inglis concluded, 'but the essential point was, and I would try to make it, that such breaches of neutrality were entirely out of character for de Valera.'

Even when there was scarcely enough petrol in the country to sustain essential services, accusations regarding the succouring of U-boats and their crews continued to appear in the foreign press and to circulate in the form of rumours at home. Cakes were allegedly being baked in Dun Laoghaire and delivered to grateful Germans in the middle of Dublin bay. The German legation in Dublin, according to the *Christian Science Monitor* (USA), had a staff of sixty. The full complement consisted, in fact, of the Minister, Edouard Hempel, and his family, Henning Thomsen, counsellor, Herr Muller and Herr Bruchhans, and two female secretaries. The only addition during the Emergency years was Carlheinz Petersen as press attache. But the fact that the Germans, Italians and Japanese continued to sustain a diplomatic presence in Ireland was enough to lead to the conviction that these missions constituted the nuclei of extensive spy networks.

Other people, of course, assumed equally that the continuing presence of British, American, Canadian and other Allied representatives argued the same conclusion, but these were not so effective in making their voices heard in Ireland. In the nature of things, and in particular because it was so much easier for native English-speakers to infiltrate the country, it was the Axis agents who attracted the most attention, particularly as they emerged as a singularly ill-starred and unhappy body of men.

Prior to the outbreak of hostilities the Germans had compiled a sizeable dossier on Ireland under the heading *Militär Geographische Ausgaben*, a work which, though apparently based on detailed reconnaissance and excellent intelligence, had its unintentional felicities. 'The great mass of the population consists', it observed, 'even today of small tenant farmers who often work quite insufficient allotments of land under very oppressive conditions . . . The houses are, especially in the West, often extremely primitive huts of broken stones with straw roofs with a few badly aired and lighted rooms in which extensive families huddle . . .' The hygienic strictures extended also to the water supply. 'The manufacture of mineral water is also widespread—it is important on account of the bad water supply in parts of the bog district.' These hazy nineteenth century fantasies seem subsequently to have permeated all the Reich's efforts to penetrate the green curtain. The few agents who succeeded in effecting a landing more or less in one piece seemed, almost to a man, to have been dispatched in a condition of woeful ignorance of things Irish. 'I knew no-one in Ireland and nobody in the High Command was able to tell me where I could best drop, as the link with the IRA was already broken', said Herman Görtz. 'Some advised me to drop anywhere in Ireland and hope for the best.' No one, for instance, had troubled to tell him that British money was acceptable in Eire. When Walter Simon landed from a U-boat in Kerry on 12/13 June he enquired politely as to the time of the next train to Tralee only to be informed that no train had run on that line (the Tralee and Dingle) for some fourteen years. Sergeant Gunther Schütz, alias Hans Marschner, arrived in the neighbourhood of New Ross, Co. Wexford with a small case containing, amongst other vital equipment, a bottle of cognac and a salami, and believing himself to be near Droichead Nua, Co. Kildare, enquired the time of the next bus to Dublin. Two gardaí escorted him to the nearest pub and hospitably plied him with Guinness until someone arrived to take him away. Three unlikely musketeers, Herren Tributh, Gärtner and Obéd, were observed plodding along a country road in the vicinity of Baltimore, West Cork on 18 July 1940. Since one of them was patently a native of the Indian sub-continent and the other two were masquerading as South Africans their mission was apparent even to the idlest of bystanders and thus was somewhat abruptly terminated. Of those apprehended only Willy Preetz, alias Paddy Mitchell, seems to have been at all well-equipped for his role. Not only did he have an Irish pseudonym, but a genuine Irish passport and an equally genuine Irish wife, and a passable Irish accent. He landed sometime in 1940 in Dingle, reached Dublin and rented a small shop in Westland Row (a favoured *quartier*, as it turned out, for those in the espionage business) from where he sent radio messages back to Germany before being apprehended. 'I fell in love with Ireland', Görtz was to confess, and a similarly sentimental approach somewhat untypical of German attitudes elsewhere at the time seems to have characterised their Irish espionage. Two professors at Deutsche Rundfunk sent forth a steady stream of propaganda broadcasts in Irish (though the *Militär Geographische Ausgaben* had stressed that 'the Irish nationalistic feeling is by no means confined to the speakers of Gaelic') and the Abwehr, who were responsible for the intelligence operations, had made the initial and understandable, though disastrous mistake, of assuming that the IRA were a fully-fledged and thoroughly professional underground organisation poised to offer them the maximum co-operation. 'The IRA's intelligence system was as primitive as that of children playing cops and robbers', Görtz was later to observe. 'They hid their messages in girls' socks—and what messages they were! There was no code—and they refused to learn even the simplest by heart. They preferred to sacrifice their men and women.' This misapprehension was paralleled in the Germans' attempt to recruit Irishmen serving with the British forces.

'An Irish brigade was to be organised from Irishmen captured in France in 1940', according to Terence Prittie, who was one of them: 'This could be used in one of two ways. It could be sent to Ireland, either to repel an Allied invasion or to take part in a German one—probably as a kind of "public relations spearhead" reassuring the Irish population during the advance as to what nice people the Nazis were. And if there were no German intrusion into Ireland, the "Irish Brigade" could be sent to Russia, to fight alongside those other unfortunate crusaders against Communism, the Spanish Blue Division . . .'

In another part of the Reich, Sam Kydd's name was read out together with those of fifty other Irishmen in Stalag 20A. They were interviewed by a Sonderführer who wanted to know why they were fighting for Britain against Germany, what their attitude would be if Ireland declared war on Britain, and whether, if repatriated, they would co-operate with the German legation in Dublin. The fact that Kydd was an Ulster Protestant and Prittie a member of the southern ascendancy (his father, he said, had been created Lord Dunalley 'for disservice to the Irish cause') seemed not to concern the authorities. Prittie was interviewed by 'a singular individual from the German Foreign Office', whose questions 'betrayed a total ignorance of the subject. I was asked about my home and about County Tipperary in general, about my own feelings towards Ireland and why, as an Irishman, I was in British uniform.'

Later, the possible recruits who had passed this initial screening were taken to a camp at Luckenwalde, some 40 kms south of Berlin, where they were treated considerably better than conventional prisoners of war. 'There were further interrogations by members of the German Foreign Office and the Abwehr', says Prittie. 'We were asked whom we regarded as "good" patriots in Ireland, and were given names when we asked, in turn, what kind of people were meant. These names were transmitted to London, and in at least two cases arrests were made subsequently in Ireland. De Valera really *did* believe in Irish neutrality and had no intention of leaving trouble-makers at large!' 'The call to defend Ireland, by being put ashore on the Irish coast, never came,' said Sam Kydd. The Irish Brigade reached a maximum strength of ten, and understandably enough in the circumstances, never went into action.

Meanwhile, the other side had not been inactive. 'Here we are in neutral Eire, dressed as fishermen . . .' reflected the captain of the *Tamura*, 'with orders to try and be attacked by U-boats . . . There were rumours that U-boats were refuelled in Ireland, that they lay up for minor repairs in deserted bays and that they landed and picked up agents. The war was very young and we were still steeped in the tradition

of World War I.' The *Tamura* was an innocent looking fishing trawler which, however, had a small submarine attached to the other end of its lines and which, in the early months of the Emergency, cheerfully invaded Irish territorial waters in search of the elusive U-boats. The risks, apart from the U-boats themselves, were the might of the Irish navy and the possibility of diplomatic embarrassment. 'During the seven or eight hours we had been inside Irish waters, Reggie's sole fear had been that we might run into the "Bogey Man" who was known to lie up river waiting to catch poachers such as we.' (Reggie was the ostensible captain of the vessel, for purposes of deception.) 'This Bogey Man was an armed fishery protection vessel, with more speed than *Tamura* and running into him would have been awkward for us all.' Their cover was nearly blown when they were forced to shelter in the lee of the Blaskets, but they were saved by the fact that two men who came off in a curragh to investigate them spoke no English. The natives in general, however, they found to be friendly, two groups who visited them off Berehaven expressing the wish that the British fleet would return, 'as in the good old days'—a sentiment no doubt stimulated by the *Tamura*'s thoughtful hospitality.

One of the many difficulties facing active and prospective agents of either interest was the attitude of the Irish authorities and the population at large. 'I did not expect that everyone in Eire would greet me with open arms', said Herman Görtz; on the other hand he contrived to stay at liberty for nineteen months, and was quite possibly apprehended by accident when, in late 1941, a house in Blackheath Park, Clontarf, Dublin was raided. (The suggestion that he was deliberately left at liberty in order to lead the authorities to his IRA associates cannot, at present, be either proved or disproved.) 'In the summer of 1941', he said, 'I was known to so many people that I began to wonder if the police were still looking for me.' At the time he was living as the respectable Mr Robinson in Dalkey, Co. Dublin, looked after by a group of ladies which included the Misses Coffey and O'Mahony and Mrs Caitlín Brugha. The latter, the widow of Cathal Brugha, also assisted Hans Marschner following his daring escape from Mountjoy prison disguised as a female on 28 February 1942. 'Who kept Hans Marschner for the eight weeks he was at large?' asked James Dillon. 'He was found in somebody's house ultimately. I know a house where he was within four days of his escape—a nursing home in this city. I suggest that the proprietress of that nursing home rang up the police and asked them to come around and collect him, and that the police reply was that they could not come.' Dillon's suggestion was somewhat wide of the mark. The Minister explained that the man was not Marschner, but another well-known to them who was subsequently arrested for obtaining board and lodging by false pretences. Marschner, immediately following his escape, had gone to a safe house in nearby Innisfallen Parade, and then, after a brief sojourn in Blackrock, Co. Dublin, to Caitlín Brugha's home, Ros na

Riogh, Temple Gardens, Rathmines. This house was raided on the very day he was planning to leave Ireland by boat, 30 April, and he was quickly back in Mountjoy, from where he was transferred, together with nine other German agents or sympathisers, to Custume Barracks, Athlone.

'In general, despite the American news media, the Irish worked with us on intelligence matters almost as if they were our allies', said J. Russell Forgan, of the Office of Strategic Services, later the CIA. 'The policy of the Special Branch was one of the clearest proofs that Ireland was "neutral for the Allies",' suggested Conor Brady. Whatever the truth of these assertions, Irish intelligence services appeared to be very well informed of the movements of Axis agents and sympathisers. A memorandum relating to the June 1940 period in General Mulcahy's papers contains the following miscellaneous particulars:

*Blunck*: 8 Dungar Terrace, Sandycove (gets large remittances from abroad).
*Hans Menhausen*: His headquarters is in Youghal—ostensibly there for his health. Travels all over south coast.
*Captain Little*: Solicitor, Middleton, Co. Cork. (ex-British army) is working with him and other Germans (Menhausen). Little's wife's sister is married to a German, believed to be in Dublin.
*Graham Picton Hughes* is apparently from Cardiff and stays at Casey's Hotel, Glengarriff. Associate of *Father Huhn*, ostensibly a refugee from Germany but apparently a 5th columnist.
*H. Martin* (or Markin?) A German on 2nd floor at No. ? South Mall, Cork. He has a pedicure business . . . from which he is frequently absent.'

There is no indication of the source of this information and no evidence of its accuracy or otherwise, but it argues that a fairly close watch was being kept. H. Martin's (or Markin's) alleged profession finds a curious echo in the case of Ernest Weber-Drohl, a former circus strong man turned chiropodist, and according to himself, a member of the European Union of Chiropractors, who was landed from U-Boat 37 some time in early February 1940. Weber-Drohl experienced the customary bad luck of his profession at the time, losing all his money and his radio getting ashore, but he succeeded in contacting the IRA in Dublin. He was arrested in a hotel in Westland Row and appeared in the Dublin District Court on 20 April 1940, where he told a fantastic story, which was at least partly true, of his having come to Ireland to seek out a lady upon whom he had fathered two children during a previous visit in his capacity as a circus performer, a Dublin chiropodist vouching for at least part of the account. He was fined £3 and released, District Justice Lennon taking the view, as he put it, 'that this man must be failing mentally to have embarked on the adventure he had undertaken'. Weber-Drohl had not, however, convinced the Special Branch, who picked him up a few days later and interned him. Some time after this, however, he was released in circumstances which remain unexplained, and tried to set up in business again, not as a chiropractor—unless he and H. Martin were one and the same person (though he gave an address at 26 Pearse Street, Dublin) but in his former role as Atlas the Strong Man with the assistance of a Miss Mary Flanagan. He was, according to himself, all set to appear at the Queen's and Theatre Royal in Dublin when Miss Flanagan withdrew her support. There is a suggestion that during this period, which lasted for about a year, he was in fact acting as a double agent, but he was arrested again and eventually joined Marschner and the others in Athlone.

When Herman Görtz parachuted to earth on 5 May 1940 in the vicinity of Ballivor, Co. Meath his introduction to Ireland was not auspicious. He failed to locate his second parachute with his radio and the spade he should have used to bury the first, and he ruined his invisible ink swimming the Boyne. He had toured the country with his wife in 1927, but that brief experience was of little assistance to him. Ladislas Farago has described him as the most inept, and even worse, the unluckiest of all spies in history, and his operation Mainau (named, with typical romanticism, after an island in Lake Constanz) as 'The Abwehr's most bird-witted project throughout the war'. Harsh criticisms, perhaps, for Görtz was intelligent, resourceful and, above all, idealistic. 'I never abandoned the hope that the progress of the war would create a situation in which the IRA might be deployed against its real objective, namely the English in Ulster', he said. His mistake was to assume that he would be playing the role of a gentleman adventurer dealing with his peers, whereas the people with whom he was to attempt to work were at best totally incompetent, and at the worst unprincipled thugs. There was, of course, plenty of thuggery about at the time, but Görtz's idealised view of the Irish struggle was not likely to be enhanced by contact with men whose idea of political action had been to blow up telephone boxes in England—and usually make a mess of it. His relationship and progressive disillusionment with the IRA ('rotten to the very core', as he was later to describe them) makes depressing reading whatever one's sympathies. He made two vain attempts to leave Ireland, one from Kerry in February 1941, the other from Brittas bay, Co. Wicklow, in August, and it was as a thoroughly disillusioned man that he began his internment in Athlone—'a small gloomy hole which, located in the middle of a barracks and surrounded by masses of barbed wire, had been converted into a real fortress'.

The internees in Custume Barracks were in a special category. The main centre of detention remained throughout the Emergency the Curragh camp ('an áit is fuaire in Éirinn go cinnte', as Mairtín O Cadhain described it) which housed, besides IRA prisoners, sailors, airmen and others from several belligerent nations who had parachuted from stricken aircraft, been picked up from shipwrecks, or had otherwise been removed, or in some cases, removed themselves, from the sphere of hostilities. The Germans were, in general, model prisoners, smartly attired in brown whipcord made to their own design by the tailors of Droichead Nua; apart from the occasional fracas (there was an incident with some Poles at a dance in Naas) their behaviour was a model of correctness and they seemed to have little inclination to attempt an escape. Not so the Allied prisoners, to whom freedom beckoned a bare seventy miles or so north. Parole was generous (daily to anywhere in the Droichead Nua–Kilcullen–Kildare area; monthly, later weekly, to Dublin) but it was understood that officers on parole would not attempt to escape. Pilot-Officer R. N. Wolfe, whose conduct on this occasion was not perhaps that of an officer and a gentleman, took off on one occasion for Belfast—from where he was promptly returned by the British authorities. On 9 February 1942 there was a mass escape attempt when 32 Allied internees overpowered the guards, who fired blank shots. The frustrated escapees later complained that excessive force had been used in restraining their attempt. A later plan, on 17 August, was more successful, three men escaping and, after having been hidden for some days by sympathizers, helped over the Border. The German internees promptly accused the guards of collusion, an accusation which might have held a grain of truth. 'It is strongly rumoured throughout the country that a number of British internees have been released and I would be very glad if the Taoiseach would confirm or deny that in order to clear up these rumours', said Oliver Flanagan in the Dáil early in 1944. 'If British internees have been released, why not release a similar number of German internees, if we are neutral?' In fact, though the Taoiseach refrained from stating it at the time, most of the Allied airforce prisoners who had fallen into Irish hands as the result of 'non-operational flights' (a generously-interpreted definition) had been released the previous October, having been moved north to Gormanston for the purpose to avoid trouble with the Axis detainees.

In the context of this covert, but nonetheless unmistakable discrimination as between two belligerent groups, the incident of the American Note in March 1944 is not without its ironic overtones. David Gray's by now pathological dislike of de Valera had determined him to do everything in his power to end the Axis representation in Dublin, and with it, as the inevitable corollary, Ireland's neutral status. The American press, by now totally intolerant of the whole concept of neutrality, was quick to respond. 'Either Eire throws out the Jap and German spies or stands the consequences', threatened the *Fort Worth Star-Telegram*. 'The snakes are back in Ireland', said the *Dallas Morning News*. Politically it was the most serious crisis of the whole period, but de Valera held firm and the agitation finally backfired on its instigator. The hard evidence was in any case, slight. Edouard Hempel, a stickler for diplomatic protocol, may possibly have had one meeting with Görtz during his active months in the country, but the majority of the German agents received little or no help from the legation, the Minister being as anxious as de Valera, though for different reasons, that nothing should be done to compromise Irish neutrality. And, in spite of wild rumours to the contrary, it is unlikely that even a modest Japanese spy network could have operated without Army and Gárda Intelligence, to say nothing of the ordinary citizen, having been aware of it.

One of the many problems besetting the spies in Ireland was that there was very little to spy on. Allied agents, such as Elizabeth Bowen was for a time, contented themselves with sounding out opinion, or, in the case of more committed individuals, attempting to influence TDs and clergymen to bring about an abandonment of neutrality. But as the war progressed even this aim became unrealistic. With the IRA either behind bars or otherwise ineffectual the Germans could do little but attempt to set up meteorological stations to beam back information of value to U-boats, though Görtz did assert, with what degree of veracity is open to question, that in the late autumn of 1941 he had established contact with a group of dissident Army officers who wanted to overthrow de Valera and invade the North. There must, in the nature of things, have been a good deal of spy versus spy activity but until and unless the relevant intelligence documents are made available any conclusions on such matters must remain in the realm of speculation.

'There was no doubt in my mind', said Görtz, 'that my sphere of action was only small, set against the pattern of the war as a whole. However, it was up to me to make something of it.' He failed, and his love-affair with Ireland ended in personal tragedy and suicide. Nor can the Allied agents, whoever and however many they may have been, have been much happier with the outcome. Espionage and subversion failed as economic and political pressure had failed in their attempts to involve the country in any compromising of its stated position. 'Mackerel', the Abwehr codeword for Eire, had indeed turned out to be a slippery customer.

"I'll teach you to say 'Please' so aggressively."

# God almighty, this exthraordinary war!

*In these six years we have, as it were in secret—not even admitting it to ourselves—come to a pretty cold and sane idea of our true natural position. It has been a deflating process, and because it has not been faced, admitted and frankly discussed, it has taken a good deal of the starch out of us . . . in our internal and external relations in the past a great part of our weakness has arisen from a ridiculously inflated, swelled-headed and unrealistic picture of our international influence and position.*

The Bell, 1945

*This country has been a non-belligerent in this terrible war. There may be room for honest differences of opinion as to whether that was or was not wise, but I do not think there is any possible room for a difference of opinion on the undoubted fact that the overwhelming majority of the people desired to keep out of the war, unless we were attacked; I heard an ex-Senator say at a meeting some time ago that neutrality was not something to boast about, but rather something to be profoundly thankful for; that is largely my own point of view.*

SENATOR JAMES DOUGLAS

WHEN THE Seanad reassembled after the Easter recess on 9 May 1945 the business placed before it was of a routine and somewhat humdrum nature. It was some time before Senators had the opportunity of referring to the event uppermost in their minds, the conclusion of the European war and thus, to all intents and purposes, of the Emergency. Eventually James Douglas rose to move a motion on Ireland's contribution to the alleviation of distress in Europe, the stark facts concerning which were only just becoming known. 'It is, I think, rather appropriate that this motion should be taken today', he said, 'when the nations that were victorious in this war are celebrating their victory, and when so many of the smaller nations are thanking God for their liberation.'

On the desperate plight of so many on the European mainland Professor Fearon had this to say: 'If any nation knows what starvation is, it is this nation. I think we have learned our history lesson. I respectfully suggest that we should learn a geography lesson also: learn that we are not an island outpost in the Atlantic, but part of the great family of nations. Justice, our geographical position and commonsense should make us appreciate that our partnership is linked up with other nations, that we are linked up with their welfare.'

'Perhaps our first consideration should be to make our contribution an act of thanksgiving', said Patrick Baxter, 'because we ourselves have been saved from all the dreadful things which the people on the Continent have suffered; in so far as we can make sacrifices now, we should be prepared to make them.'

Thanksgiving—or remorse born of guilt? 'We have suffered by the prolonged suppression of our natural sympathies with tortured humanity', wrote Seán O Faoláin, 'our admiration for endurance and courage, our moral judgements have been in abeyance; our intellectual interest in all the ideas and problems which the rest of the world is still straining to solve have been starved.'

There are more questions than there are answers: did neutrality indefinitely postpone Irish reunification, or simply confirm an existing situation? Did the country emerge morally the poorer for the experience? For some, Mr de Valera's courtesy call on the German Minister to express his condolences on the death of Hitler was the last straw: 'Considering the character and record of the man for whom he was expressing grief there is obviously something wrong with the protocol, the neutrality, or Mr de Valera,' wrote the *New York Times*. The reaction was predictable, as was Churchill's notorious attack. The moral issues, to the victors, seemed crystal clear—for the moment. There was no room for shades of grey.

Any six year period, even one as traumatic as the years 1939–45, is in one sense an arbitrary imposition on history, in that it is possible to argue that there were continuing elements in Irish life and culture which remained largely unmoved by what was happening in the theatres of war: the role of religion, the preoccupation with the language, the sexual and matrimonial patterns born of the structure and organisation of society. Any invasion, of course, would have had a profound effect on most or all of these elements. Or would it? The posing of this extreme hypothetical question is merely to exemplify the futility of trying to reach conclusions as to the abstract outcome of the Emergency experience. The arguments over morality and expediency will continue, but in the meantime there is room for some more positive assessment.

A number of practical steps were taken during the period, whether voluntarily or under pressure of circumstances, which have had far-reaching consequences—political, economic, social and cultural. Some of these have been referred to in some detail: the establishment, after years of neglect, of a merchant marine; the development of Shannon as a major international airport. The need to exploit turf resources led directly to the emergence of Bord na Mona as one of the most enterprising and successful of post-war Semi-State Bodies. The setting up of the Dublin Institute of Advanced Studies, besides offering congenial refuge to some very distinguished intellectuals, created an institution that has since won itself a reputation in several fields. Art, music, literature, in both Irish and English, far from being stifled by isolationism, showed themselves to be very much alive, in spite of, or perhaps because of, the conditions prevailing.

Against this one must set the admitted stagnation in political and social development during and after the Emergency, though how far this can be attributed to the specific conditions of neutrality is difficult to assess. Probably the greatest single gain, however, was in national self-awareness, a coming-of-age which, if at times tending to manifest itself in traditional forms of self-denigration and the béal bocht, introduced a new note of reality and underlying self-confidence which laid the foundations for Seán Lemass's successful pragmatism of the 'sixties.

The old ambivalences remained—the ambivalences which beset a small society, a relatively poor society, a society still subject to the stresses imposed by divergent traditions. If perhaps the greatest single effect of neutrality was to add a few miles to the distance across the Irish sea and achieve through exigency a measure of economic and political independence of action that might have been very slow to manifest itself under normal conditions (the maritime situation is a case in point) it by no means succeeded at arriving at a new definition of the Anglo-Irish relationship, the most complex ambiguity of them all. This was nowhere more succinctly exemplified than in some verses by Michael Matthews which appeared under the title of *Moryah* in the 9 March 1944 issue of *TCD*:

Would you talk a little less about O'Connell?
Have you finished quoting from 'The Great O'Neill'?

Do you realise that Tone
*Never* kissed the Blarney Stone
And that Parnell was deficient in appeal?

What, you did your Christmas shopping through the medium?
You were under your O'Dearest in '16?
You are intimate and pally
with Professor Alf O'Rahilly,
And you hate the sight of Senator John Keane?

You were born just forty paces from McBirney's?
You think 2RN should keep the ether clean?
That we'd be a nation sooner
If we bumped off every crooner
And danced sets around Tom Moore in College Green?

You're a decent bowsy after my own heart then;
Come and have a couple up in Inchicore!
*What! You're building tanks in Jarrow*
*And your leave is up tomorrow?*
God Almighty, this *exthraordinary* war!

## SELECT BIBLIOGRAPHY

This bibliography is restricted to primary sources which have been drawn upon for close reference or direct quotation as indicated in the text. Verbal and other indirect sources are acknowledged elsewhere.

PUBLISHED SOURCES

ARNOLD, R. M., *The Golden Years of the Great Northern Railway*, Belfast 1976
    *Athlone Step Together Week: souvenir brochure*, Athlone 1942

BAKER, M. H. C., *Irish Railways since 1916*, London 1972
BARDWELL, LELAND, *Girl on a Bicycle*, Dublin 1977
*Barrack Variety*, Dublin 1942–43
*Barr Buadh, An*, Cork 1943–45
*Bell, The*, Dublin 1940–45
BOWEN, ELIZABETH, *The Shelbourne*, London 1951
BRADY, CONOR, *Guardians of the Peace*, Dublin 1974
BROMAGE, MARY C., *Churchill and Ireland*, Notre Dame 1964

*Call to Arms, The*, Dublin 1945
CAMPBELL, PATRICK, *An Irishman's diary*, London 1951
    *My life and easy times*, London 1967
CARROLL, J. T., *Ireland in the War Years, 1939–45*, Newton Abbott 1975
CONWAY, NOEL, *The Bloods: the first 50 years of the Third Infantry Battalion*, Dublin 1974
COOGAN, T. P., *The I.R.A.*, London 1970
COX, COLM, 'Militär geographische ausgaben über Irland. *An Cosantóir*, March 1975
*Curragh Bulletin*, Curragh Camp 1940–45
CURRIVAN, P. J., 'Engineman's son', *Journal of the Irish Railway Record Society*, 1975

*Dublin Opinion*, Dublin 1939–45
DWYER, T. RYLE, 'Benevolent internment', *An Cosantóir*, June 1977
    *Irish neutrality and the U.S.A., 1939–47*, Dublin 1977

FARAGO, LADISLAS, *The Game of Foxes*, New York 1971

FELL, W. R., *The Sea our Shield*, London 1966

FOLEY, DONAL, *Three Villages*, Dublin 1977

FORDE, FRANK, 'Convoy OG 74 and s.s. "City of Waterford" ', *An Cosantóir*, June 1977

'm.v. "Kerlogue" of Wexford in World War Two', *An Cosantóir*, December 1977


GLENDINNING, VICTORIA, *Elizabeth Bowen: Portrait of a Writer*, London 1977

GORHAM, MAURICE, *Forty Years of Irish Broadcasting*, Dublin 1967

GRAHAM, MARY, *Ring the Doctor*, Dublin 1967

GREACEN, ROBERT, *Even without Irene*, Dublin 1969


INGLIS, BRIAN, *West Briton*, London 1962

*Irish Army Pictorial*, Dublin 1943

*Irish Defence Forces Handbook*, Dublin 1974


KEARNS, A. P., 'Flight to Rineanna', *An Cosantóir*, September 1972

Off-course landings and crashes: World War II, *An Cosantóir*, June 1977

KYDD, SAM, *For you the war is over ...*, London 1973


LAFFAN, J., 'The Army serum production centre in World War II', *An Cosantóir*, April 1975

*Leader, The*, Dublin 1939–45

LONGFORD, EARL OF, and O'NEILL, THOMAS P., *Eamon de Valera*, Dublin and London 1970

*L.S.F. Gazette*, Dublin 1940–45

LYONS, F. S. L., *Ireland since the Famine*, London 1971


McCARTHY, DENIS J., 'Armour in the War Years', *An Cosantóir*, March 1975

McDONAGH, OLIVER, *The Union and its Aftermath*, London 1976

McDONALD, J. G., 'The Army Ordnance Corps', *An Cosantóir*, March 1977

MacKENNA, T., 'Thank God we're surrounded by water', *An Cosantóir*, April 1973

McREDMOND, L. (ed.), *Written on the wind*, Dublin 1976

MacTHOMAIS, EAMONN, *Gur cakes and coal blocks*, Dublin 1976

MOFFETT, MARGARET, 'Young Irish painters', *Horizon*, April 1945
MULCAHY, J. and YOUNG, J., '11th Field Co. S. & T.', *An Cosantóir*, June 1975

NOLAN, KEVIN B. and WILLIAMS, T. DESMOND, *Ireland in the War Years and After*, Dublin 1969

O'BEIRNE, MICHAEL, 'A month on the bog', *The Bell*, March 1943
Ó BRIÁIN, E., 'The 11th Motor Squadron', *An Cosantóir*, January 1976
Ó CADHAIN, MAIRTIN, *As an nGéibheann*, Baile Atha Cliath 1973
O'KEEFFE, T. (ed,), *Myles: portraits of Brian O'Nolan*, London 1973
Ó NÉILL, EOGHAN, 'The Construction Corps', *An Cosantóir*, November 1977

*Passing Variety*, Dublin 1943–45
PETERSON, BASIL, *Turn of the tide*, Dublin 1962
PRITTIE, TERENCE, *Through Irish eyes*, London 1977

QUIGLEY, AIDAN A., *The Story of an Irish Jet Pilot*, Dublin and Cork 1976

RYAN, JOHN, *Remembering how we stood*, Dublin 1975

*Spearhead, The (Sleagh ar aghaidh)*, Curragh Camp 1942–45

*T.C.D., a College miscellany*, Dublin 1939–45
THOMPSON, DAVID, *Woodbrook*, London 1974

VAN HOEK, KEES, *Country of my choice*, Tralee 1945
                  *Diplomats in Dublin*, Dublin 1944
Various, *Eamon de Valera: a survey by the 'Irish Times'*, Dublin 1976

WHITE, MARTIN, '*Fifty years of a loco man's life*' (*Journal of the Irish Railway Record Society*, 1963)


SPECIFIC UNPUBLISHED SOURCES

FLEETWOOD, JOHN and WALKER, VINCENT, *Recollections of the L.S.F.*
MULCAHY, RICHARD, Private papers in the archive of University College, Dublin


GENERAL

Dáil and Seanad reports; national and provincial newspapers, 1939–45